O9-BUB-861

AN ANCHOR
for the
SOUL

AN ANCHOR
for the
SOUL

HELP
FOR THE
PRESENT,
HOPE
FOR THE
FUTURE

RAY PRITCHARD

© 2000 by
RAY PRITCHARD

All rights reserved. No part of this book may be reproduced in any form without permission in writing from the publisher, except in the case of brief quotations embodied in critical articles or reviews.

All Scripture quotations, unless otherwise indicated, are taken from the Holy Bible, New International Version®. NIV®. Copyright © 1973, 1978, 1984 by International Bible Society. Used by permission of Zondervan Publishing House. All rights reserved.

Scripture quotations marked NASB are taken from the *New American Standard Bible®*, © Copyright The Lockman Foundation 1960, 1962, 1963, 1968, 1971, 1972, 1973, 1975, 1977, 1995. Used by permission.

Scripture quotations marked NKJV are taken from the *New King James Version*. Copyright © 1982 by Thomas Nelson, Inc. Used by permission. All rights reserved.

ISBN: 0-8024-1535-0

7 9 10 8

Printed in the United States of America

In memory of
Gary Olson
He loved to tell the story.
How beautiful upon the mountains are the feet
of him who brings good news.
Isaiah 52:7 NKJV

TABLE OF CONTENTS

INTRODUCTION

This book is written for people who want to know God. If that describes you, then I have some good news for you. It is possible for you to know God deeply and personally, and by knowing God, you can experience His power in your life.

This good news doesn't come from me. It comes from God Himself. In the Bible this good news is called the "gospel." The gospel is good news because it tells what God has done so that men and women can come into a personal relationship with the One who made them.

Everything in this book is based on two facts. First, you were made to know God, and you can't and won't be truly satisfied until you know Him. Nothing this world offers can take the place of knowing God. Second, the Bible tells us how we can know God personally. The Bible does not tell us everything we could know on every subject, but it tells us everything we need to know about being right with God. It only makes sense that the God who made us knows us better than we know ourselves. And we need to hear what He has to say. I'm not going to quote many Scripture verses in this book, but the things I write are all based on what the Bible says.

Let me say right up front that this book will be helpful no matter where you might be on your spiritual journey. When it comes to knowing God, we all stand in different places. Some are seekers, some are doubters, some are skeptics, and some know very little about the Christian faith. Others were raised in a church but drifted away years ago.

If you would like to know God, that's all that matters. You may count yourself as a religious person, or you may think of yourself as nonreligious. That's fine either way. Many people today have a deep interest in spiritual matters, even though they are not part of any religious organization. If that describes you, I hope you'll read this book carefully because I am writing to you as an individual in order to help you find a personal relationship with God.

I'm sure you have a few questions. I hope so, because honest questions deserve good answers. Here are some questions you may have:

> What is God like?
>
> How can I know Him?
>
> Am I really a sinner?
>
> How can my sins be forgiven?
>
> Who is Jesus, and what did He do?
>
> What must I do to be saved?
>
> What does it mean to be a Christian?
>
> How can I find peace with God?
>
> How can I be sure I am going to heaven?

The story of the Bible is good news that can change your life. It tells us about ourselves, our deepest problems, and God's amazing solution to those problems. More than that, it presents to us the person of Jesus Christ and describes the new life He offers to one and all. This is the supreme message of the Bible. Even if you have doubts or questions about the Bible, I encourage you to read with an open mind and then decide for yourself about what I've written.

It's entirely possible that you are a bit skeptical about the whole concept of knowing God. Perhaps you've been turned off by organized religion or by certain Christians whose words or deeds don't seem to match up with what they claim to believe. While I freely admit that Christians sometimes can be the worst advertisement for their faith, I hope you'll set aside your preconceptions as you read this book.

If you are not disposed to believe in Jesus, nothing in this book will convince you to change your mind. Since spiritual reality is a matter of perception and not proof, I don't believe in trying to argue people into the Christian faith. The Bible says that no one comes to God unless the Father draws him through the Spirit. So if you're a skeptic, don't worry; you won't be converted against your will by reading this book.

On the other hand, this book could change your life. If the gospel is truly good news from God, then we shouldn't be surprised if our lives are radically changed as we come to know God personally through the Lord Jesus Christ.

But I'm getting a bit ahead of myself. All we know so far is that this book contains good news that comes from God as revealed in the Bible. For the rest of the story, you'll need to read each chapter slowly and think about what it says. At this point I'd like to suggest a simple prayer for spiritual guidance. I encourage you to read this prayer slowly, phrase by phrase. If it expresses the desire of your heart, pray it quietly to God.

> *O God, I want to know You. If You are really there, please reveal Yourself to me. Show me the truth about myself. Open my eyes and create faith in my heart. Give me the gift of an open mind to receive Your truth. Speak to me through what I read, that I may come to know You. Grant that my deepest questions may be answered with Your truth. Help me to seek You with all my heart. And may I find You and be satisfied with what I find. Amen.*

You needn't be fearful about praying a prayer like this because God never turns any honest seeker away. If you seek the Lord with all your heart you will find Him. You might want to put your initials and today's date by that prayer if it expresses the desire of your heart.

Now it's time to begin. The first step in knowing God is finding out more about who He really is.

Chapter One

A PLACE
TO BEGIN

Suppose I say to you, "Define God in twenty words or less." And I give you thirty seconds to do it. What would you say? Could you do it? Does it seem unfair? Suppose I give you 200,000 words and thirty years. Would it be any easier? And would you come any closer to the truth?

God is the first fundamental of the universe, which is why we can't really "define" Him. But we can say this: knowing God is the most important thing in life. If you live thirty or forty or fifty or sixty or seventy or eighty years and you don't know God, then it doesn't matter what else you have done with your life. If you don't know God, you have missed the very reason for your own existence. If you miss out on knowing God, you have missed the central reality of the universe. Compared to knowing the One who made you, everything else is just crumbs and nibbling around the edges.

OUR NEED—
TO KNOW THE GOD WHO MADE US

We were made to know God, and something in us desperately wants to know Him. We are incurably religious by nature. That's why every human society—no matter how primitive—has some concept of a higher power, some vision of a reality that goes beyond the natural. On one level, that explains why science has not eradicated religion from the earth. Science can never do that because technological achievement can't meet the deepest needs of the human heart. That explains why millions of people read their horoscopes every morning and millions more call psychic hotlines.

We want to know the answers to the three most basic questions of life: *Where did I come from? Why am I here? Where am I going?* And we will spend money, buy books, listen to tapes, attend seminars, and travel great distances to find the answers. Several years ago a book claiming to report one woman's after-death visit to heaven climbed to the top of the best-seller list. Recently another book purporting to find hidden messages in the Hebrew text of the Old Testament sold hundreds of thousands of copies. People are hungry for spiritual truth, and if they cannot find it by normal means, they will reach for anyone or anything that claims to give them an answer.

It is the same wherever you travel. Superficially we are very different in our appearance, background, language, and customs. But scratch deeper, and you discover that all people are substantially the same. Once past the surface, you discover no fundamental difference between a person born in poverty in Haiti and a corporate lawyer on Wall Street; or between a schoolteacher in Addis Ababa, Ethiopia, and a computer scientist in Singapore. Everywhere we are the same—with the same longings, regrets, dreams, and hopes; with the same need to love and be loved; with the same desire to be remembered after we die; and with the same sense that there must be a God of some kind who made us.

We were made to know God, and we need to know Him. God made us to know Him. He designed us so that we would want to know Him—and then He guaranteed we wouldn't be happy unless He Himself fills the void within. This brings us face-to-face with the famous statement that there is a "God-shaped vacuum" inside each person. We may turn to God, or we may fill the vacuum with idols of our own making or the evil spirits of our ancestors. Something in us drives us to seek ultimate meaning. That "something" inside us is put there by God. Augustine gave us this oft-quoted prayer: "You have made us for yourself, and our hearts are restless until they find their rest in you."

GOD'S DESIRE—
THAT WE SHOULD KNOW HIM

The whole Bible demonstrates that God wants us to know Him. In a sense, that is the theme of the Bible—how God loved us, how we rebelled against Him, and how God set about rescuing people who had turned against Him. The story is clear enough. God sent prophets, priests, and messengers of various sorts. He sent His messages in writing. But we (the human race) didn't want anything to do with God. So we ignored His message and sometimes killed His messengers. Then He sent His Son, Jesus Christ, the ultimate expression of His love. And we killed Him, too. But in His death God made a way for anyone and everyone to be forgiven.

Let's go back to the very beginning of the story for a moment. When God first created the world, He created Adam and Eve and made them "in his image" and "after his likeness." These simple phrases are full of meaning for us. We were made in God's image, which means there is something in us that corresponds to who God is. You and I were designed to know God personally. Dogs don't pray, birds don't worship, fish don't praise—but we do. Why? Because there is a "God-consciousness" inside every human heart. It is that "God-consciousness" that makes us want to know God and makes us eager to find out why we exist.

FATHER HUNGER

But there's another part of the story. Ever since Adam and Eve sinned in the Garden of Eden, that image of God within each of us has been marred by sin. I picture a piece of paper with the words GOD'S IMAGE in huge letters. Before Adam and Eve sinned, that paper was clean and smooth. But now for all of us that paper is crumpled, dirty, and torn. But it is never completely destroyed. Despite all our failures, we still want to know God, and we still want to find meaning in life but just don't know where to look.

To use a very modern phrase, we are left with a kind of "Father hunger." That's a phrase used to describe children growing up in a family without a strong and compassionate father figure. He may have died or he may have abandoned his family. Or perhaps he was so busy he had no time for his family. Because he barely knows his children, they compete desperately for his little scraps of love and approval. Children growing up in a home like that desperately want a father, and sometimes they will look for someone (or something) to fill that void.

On a much larger scale, that's the story of all humanity. We were made to know God and we want to know Him, but our sin has separated us from God. As a result, we are left with a deep "Father hunger" that won't seem to go away.

OUR SEARCH—IN ALL THE WRONG PLACES

So what do we do? As a popular song says, we

look for love in all the wrong places. We can illustrate this using a pen and a piece of paper. Draw a cliff on the right side of the paper and label it "God." On the left side draw a cliff and label it "Us." Label the gap in between with the word "Sin." That's the problem we all face. We're on one side, God is on the other, and our sin stands between God and us. Something deep inside tells us we belong on the other side with the God who made us. So we set out to build bridges across the great chasm.

Now draw lines that start on the "Us" side and move toward the "God" side, ending each line somewhere in-between the two cliffs. Each line represents a human "bridge" we build in our attempts to find our way back to God. One bridge is labeled "Money," another "Education," another "Good works," another "Sex," another "Power," another "Science," another "Success," another "Approval," another "Relationships," and another "Religion." You can make as many bridges as you like, but they never seem to reach the other side. Each one ends somewhere in the middle, illustrating the truth that you can never find God by starting where you are. No matter which road you take, you fall into the great chasm and end up being broken on the jagged rocks of reality.

That's what I mean by "searching in all the wrong places." Nothing in this world can satisfy our longing because nothing in this world can lead us back to God. The answer we need must come from outside this world.

Three thousand years ago, a wise man named

Solomon went on a search to find the key to the meaning of life. He recorded his findings in a book of the Bible called Ecclesiastes. In the first two chapters he tells about his grand experiment. He built buildings, planted vast gardens, tried the party scene, and accumulated a vast fortune. He gathered books and amassed a vast store of human knowledge. Anything he wanted, he got for himself. Nothing was held back. He tried anything and everything in his search for meaning.

He reported his finding in three terse words: "I hated life" (Ecclesiastes 2:17). When nothing satisfies, when you've truly tried it all, when you can say with calm assurance, "Been there, done that" and you still feel the emptiness within, what do you do then? Solomon's conclusion could stand as an epitaph for every generation.

Here is our problem in a nutshell. We were made by God to know God. There is a "God-shaped vacuum" inside each person that causes us to seek after the One who made us. Because we search in all the wrong places, we can never find Him. Our eternal longing for God is not fulfilled.

GOD'S SOLUTION—
HE HAS MADE HIMSELF KNOWN

In the end we are left with this great truth: We can never know God unless He reveals Himself to us. Try as we might we always end up in the darkness, seeking a God we know is there but cannot seem to find. But God has not left us to live in darkness forever. He has revealed Himself in four primary ways:

A. In *creation*—Everyone sees this.

B. In *the human conscience*—Everyone has this.

C. In *His written Word, the Bible*—Not everyone knows this.

D. In *His Son, Jesus Christ*—Not everyone understands this.

The last revelation is the most important. Jesus is "God incarnate," that is, God clothed with human flesh. When Jesus walked on the earth, He was the God-man, fully God and fully man at the same time. Jesus is the supreme revelation of God. If you've seen Jesus, you've seen God. If you want to know what God is like, look at Jesus.

SOME FACTS ABOUT GOD

The Bible says a great deal about who God is and how He has revealed Himself. Here are six facts about God you need to know:

1. He eternally exists in three persons

The truth about God begins with the fact that He eternally exists as the Father, the Son, and the Holy Spirit. When we say that, we mean that the Father is God, the Son is God, and the Holy Spirit is God, but they are not three gods but only one God. The Father is not the Son, the Son is not the Spirit, the Spirit is not the Father, but each is God individually and yet they are together the one true God of the Bible. This is called the doctrine of the Holy Trinity.

Someone asked Daniel Webster, who happened to be a fervent Christian, "How can a man of your intellect believe in the Trinity?" "I do not pretend fully to understand the arithmetic of heaven now," he replied. That's a good phrase—*the arithmetic of heaven*.

The Trinity should cause us to bow in humble adoration before a God who is greater than our minds could ever comprehend. We have a God who has provided everything necessary for our salvation. When we were lost in sin, our God acted in every person of His being to save us. The Father gave the Son, the Son offered Himself on the cross, and the Holy Spirit draws us to Jesus.

2. He is the Sovereign Lord

God is the purest, simplest, most basic being in the universe. He is a personal God—not an impersonal force. Because He is infinite, He is not subject to time, corruption, or decay. Because He is eternal, He is always present everywhere in the universe. He is the "unmoved mover," "the uncaused first cause," and the source of all that is. He is the power behind all other power.

His character is unchanging—and therefore entirely dependable. What He says, He will do. Because He has the only truly "free will" in the universe, He does whatever He pleases, yet He never acts in an arbitrary fashion, but only in conformity with His own perfect character.

God is holy, which means He is utterly pure, free from all evil, totally without blame or error. Holiness is what makes God God. He never lowers His standards, never compromises, and makes no "deals." All that He does is right, just, and good. There is no falsehood in Him or from Him. He makes the rules, and no one can object. He Himself is the final standard of right and wrong. Therefore, everything He says about you and me is true.

3. He created all things

God designed everything that is; He initiated Creation and personally brought all things into being. The universe did not happen by chance, accident, or by the random collision of cells. It is not the product of random evolution. God spoke and the universe came into being. He is so powerful that He is the source of all things—living and nonliving. All things were made by Him, and all things exist at this moment by His powerful word. This means that He personally created you, that you were put on this earth for a reason, and that the highest purpose of your life is to know the God who made you. Think about that for a moment. The God who can create anything—created you! And He wants you to know Him personally.

4. He made you in His image

You were made to know God. Something in you yearns to know the God who created you. That yearning may be hidden deep within, or you may feel it burning inside you at this moment. Perhaps you have tried to cover it up or to satisfy your longings with the things of this world. But that doesn't work. You were made with desires that nothing in this world can satisfy. Only God can fill the hole in your heart. Only God can love you the way you long to be loved.

5. He knows all about you

Theologians call this "omniscience," which simply means that God knows everything—the past, the present, and the future. He is never caught by surprise by anything that happens anywhere in the universe. Nothing is hidden from Him. That includes your secret thoughts, your dreams, and your unfulfilled desires. He knows your words before you speak them and your thoughts before you think them. He knows where you were last night and who you were with. He knows the whole story of your life— the good, the bad, and the ugly. What about those secret things that no one else knows about? He knows them all, and He knows them completely.

6. He cares about you

The Bible tells us that "God is love." He is perfect, infinite, unconditional love. His love is freely given. It is not a reward for good behavior because no one can ever "earn" God's love. The greatest gifts in life are the ones we don't deserve. No gift could be greater than the love of God. The Bible declares that God loves the unlovely. We shook our fists at God and sinned against Him. The amazing news is that God even loves His enemies. While we were sinners, God demonstrated His love by sending His Son to the earth to die for us.

We need to know a God who loves us like that. To miss knowing this God is to miss the central truth of the universe. It's like visiting Rome and seeing everything but St. Peter's Square. It's like traveling to Washington, D.C., and seeing everything but the White House. It's like going to Paris and seeing everything but the Eiffel Tower. Or it's like going to the Super Bowl and watching everything but the football game.

THE ONLY THING THAT MATTERS IS GOD

Let's wrap up this chapter with a story about a young man I knew who was only twenty-six years old when he died. Although he grew up in a Christian home, during his teens and early twenties he went through a period of rebellion and spiritual searching. His life changed when the doctors discovered a brain tumor. Surgery brought a brief remission, and then the cancer returned.

As the months passed, his faith increased even as his physical condition worsened. He began to seek the Lord as never before. The Word of God became sweet to him. He became bold in his witness, especially to his many friends. He asked God to use him to reach others so that he could point people to Christ, no matter how long he lived.

During the funeral, his younger sister talked about how much she loved him, how as a young girl she wanted to be like him, and how exasperating he could be at times. Then the cancer came. She saw a difference so profound that it changed everything. Her brother had figured out what life is all about. Then she said this sentence: *Life is nothing without God.* He had shown her that it doesn't matter how long you live or how much money you have or even how well you do in your career. His faith at the end spoke one simple message: Life is nothing without God. She marveled that someone so young—her brother—had figured out the meaning of life. And she thanked him for leaving her with that all-important truth: Life is nothing without God.

When I stood up to deliver the message a few minutes later, I didn't have to say very much. I simply repeated what she said one more time: *Life is nothing without God.*

I then made this application. If you live for eighty years but don't discover that truth, you've missed the very reason for your own existence. If you should earn a million dollars—or $10 million—and have hundreds of friends and the praise of your contemporaries, if you have all that but don't figure out this basic truth, you're still in spiritual kindergarten.

Have you discovered what life is all about? Life is nothing without God. Everything else is just details.

Knowing the God who made you is the most important thing in life. It gives meaning and purpose to
everything else. If you don't know God, nothing else
matters.

So the question we need to ask is this: *Do you know
God, and if you don't, would you like to know Him?* The
good news is, you can know Him. But before we can
get to the good news, we have to face the bad news.
And that's what the next chapter is all about.

Chapter Two

THE TRUTH ABOUT YOU

A few years ago a friend passed along a clipping from a local paper regarding an odd bit of information tucked away in the obituaries (*Chicago Tribune*, 25 February 1992). It seems that "Wally the Wiretapper" had died. Normally that wouldn't rate any special attention, but as I read the clipping, I realized that "Wally the Wiretapper" was no ordinary crook.

The obituary called him a "fabled Chicago felon" who engaged in a "variety of crime as a Damon Runyon-like character." He freely admitted to tapping phones for his clients, who included various well-known mobsters. He evidently was good at what he did. During his criminal career, he had been convicted of, among other things, defrauding insurance companies; posing as a federal agent; and past-posting horse races, which means he used electronic equipment to place bets on races that had already been run in other cities (that's the scheme Paul Newman and Robert Redford pulled off in the movie *The Sting*).

At one point in his long career, he was approached by certain Hollywood types who wanted to make a movie about his life. But he was persuaded not to go along when his friends in the mob gently discussed the matter with him. "My friends in the mob," he said, "asked how I was going to spend the movie profits if I was six feet down. I got the message, and I said good-bye to the Hollywood screenwriter."

I was attracted to his story when I learned his real name—Walter Dewey Pritchard. When Mr. Pritchard was sentenced in 1984 after being convicted of interstate racketeering, the presiding judge made a telling comment. "I see no redeeming features for Mr. Pritchard at all, except that he's a nice guy." It made me wonder if Wally and I don't share the same family tree. As far as I know there is no direct connection, but I'll bet if you go back far enough, you would discover that he's really my uncle, four times removed.

That wasn't the end of my reflection. As I pondered the matter, I realized that story could have been written about me. "Uncle" Wally and I have more in common than I would like to admit. A little more reflection led me to an unnerving conclusion: What the judge said about Wally the Wiretapper, he could have said about me: "I see no redeeming features for Mr. Pritchard at all, except that he's a nice guy." From a biblical standpoint, that's a perfectly accurate statement. There are no redeeming features in me.

WHATEVER BECAME OF SIN?

Lest this self-assessment seem overly harsh, consider the words of G. K. Chesterton: "Whatever else is or is not true, this one thing is certain—man is not what he was meant to be." I'm sure I don't need to spend a great deal of time debating that point. If you have any question about the sinfulness of the human race, go anywhere in the world, pick up any newspaper you want, in any language you please. Simply read the front page and you will be convinced.

A quarter-century ago, psychiatrist Karl Menninger wrote a landmark book titled *Whatever Became of Sin?* There are many answers to that question, but this one is certainly true. Nothing has happened to sin, but something has happened to us. We simply don't want to talk about sin anymore. It isn't a polite topic, especially not in polite society. Try mentioning the word *sin* the next time you go to a party and see how long it takes for someone to change the subject.

But our avoiding the subject doesn't change the truth. Something has gone wrong with the human race. No one can successfully deny that fact. We are not all that we could be. And no matter how much we boast of our technological achievements, the fact of man's inhumanity to man always grabs the front page. The details change, the faces come and go, but the story is always the same. Something evil lurks inside the heart of every person. No one is immune, no one is exempt, and no one is truly innocent.

Call it what you will—a twist, a taint, a bent to do wrong. Somehow, somewhere, someone injected poison into the human bloodstream. That's why, even when we know the right thing to do, we often go ahead and choose to do what is wrong. Deliberately. Repeatedly. Defiantly.

The world is a mess—we all know that. The world is a mess because we ourselves are messed up. The problem is not "out there." It's "in us." The world is bad because we are bad. The world is evil because evil lurks within us.

DON'T FORGET TO LOCK YOUR CAR

It is common today to talk about evil as a result of a bad environment, lack of education, and poverty. Many people believe that if only those things could be changed, we could eradicate evil in the world. We hope to change people by changing their environment. After billions and billions of dollars, it hasn't happened, and it won't happen. Today we have produced a generation of high-tech criminals who know how to kill more people with less effort than ever before. Racism remains, killing continues, crime spreads, and nations are still at war. Ethnic violence seems to be the order of the day. Why? Because there is evil inside the human heart.

Not long ago I asked my congregation how many

people locked the doors to their homes and cars before coming inside the church. The answer was, almost everyone. We have elaborate security systems because human nature has not been improved.

Our problem is sin that separates us from God. We call it by other names, whitewash it, and then relabel it. But it doesn't work. You can take a bottle of rat poison and label it Orange Juice but that doesn't change its basic character. If you drink it, you will die. Poison is still poison, no matter what you call it.

THE NATURE OF SIN

What is sin? It is any violation of God's righteous character. It is anything we say or do or think or imagine or plan that does not meet God's standard of perfection. The Bible uses many word pictures to describe sin:

Sin is *lawlessness*. That means sin is anything that ignores or violates the standard God laid down in the Bible.

Sin is *missing the mark*. Picture an archer shooting an arrow and missing so badly that not only does he not hit the bull's-eye, he doesn't even hit anywhere on the target. Sin causes us to aim our lives in the wrong direction and to miss the mark of what God wants us to do and to be.

Sin is *transgression*. This means going beyond the limits of what God has said is good and proper.

Sin is *iniquity*. This is a stronger word that means deliberately choosing to do wrong. It has within it the idea of premeditated disobedience.

Sin is *deviation from the standard*. This describes a crookedness of the soul that results in a life full of twisted choices, evil deeds, and broken relationships.

Sin touches the inner ugliness of the soul. It involves our thoughts, our dreams, and our hidden motivations seen by no one else. But God sees everything. So much takes place beneath the surface. We can hide from others, and even hide from ourselves, but we cannot hide from God. All things are laid bare before His all-seeing eyes.

The Bible traces sin back to the Garden of Eden. God told Adam and Eve not to eat of the fruit of one particular tree. The serpent deceived Eve, who ate the fruit and then offered some to Adam who, though he was not deceived, ate the fruit anyway. It was through that deliberate choice that sin entered the world. Before that moment he was a living soul in an immortal body. After that moment he was a dead soul in a dying body. If you had been there that day, all you would have seen was a man taking fruit from his wife and eating it. No lightning, no thunder, no bells, no scary music in the background. Yet from that one act of disobedience, disastrous results flowed out across history.

Theologians call this event "The Fall." It means that when Adam ate the fruit he fell from a state of innocence into a state of guilt. He fell from grace to judgment. He fell from life to death.

ADAM DROVE THE BUS OFF THE CLIFF

What does all this have to do with you and me? In some mysterious way, you and I were there. When Adam sinned, you sinned with him and so did I. This is the doctrine of original sin in its plainest form. It means that when Adam sinned, you sinned. When Adam disobeyed, you disobeyed. When Adam fell, you fell. When he died, you died. To say it another way, although you and I were not historically there in the garden, because we are descendents of Adam—part of his family tree—we suffer the consequences of what he did.

Let me say it another way. Adam was the driver of the bus of humanity. When he drove the bus over the cliff, we went down with him. Or you could say he was at the controls when the plane crashed. It doesn't matter that we were back in the coach section watching a movie. When he crashed, we all went up in flames.

A few years ago, the great tennis player Arthur Ashe died of AIDS contracted through tainted blood given to him during heart surgery. He didn't know it, the doctors didn't know it, nobody intended for it to happen. But when that blood was pumped into Arthur Ashe, it contained the deadly AIDS virus. Nothing could be done about it. Eventually the disease he contracted through tainted blood took his life.

When Adam sinned, he tainted the human bloodstream. The virus of sin entered the human bloodstream, and as a result, every baby born into this world is tainted with the deadly sin virus. Every person is born with a tendency to do wrong. We're all born with a sin nature.

We may not like to face this truth about ourselves, and we may protest that we had nothing to do with Adam's sin. A friend told me that his father has gout and three of the sons also have gout. He said his father often jokingly remarked to his boys, "You didn't choose your parents very well." But we don't choose our parents—physically or spiritually. We had nothing to do with the physical characteristics we inherited from our parents. Likewise, we inherited a sin nature from Adam because, if you trace the record back far enough, he is at the root of every family tree in the whole human race.

Many people think God has some kind of divine voltmeter that registers "Good," "Neutral," and "Evil." They think that by nature the needle that measures their soul is somewhere right in the middle—not too bad, not too good, mostly just neutral. They aren't the best, but they aren't the worst either. But the Bible tells us that because of Adam's sin we come into the world with the needle stuck firmly on "Evil." Apart from the grace of God, that's where the needle will stay as long as we live.

You're not evil because you *do* evil. You do evil because you *are* evil. Your basic nature is corrupt and depraved. That's your inheritance from Adam. You are born living on the Wild Side. You are born with a minus on your record. You turned the wrong way back in the garden and you've been going the wrong way ever since.

It started with Adam, but it didn't end there. It continues in your life and in mine. Adam was the first sinner, but he wasn't the last. We follow in the footsteps of our forefather because we share his tainted blood.

IF SIN WERE BLUE

I can imagine someone reading to this point and saying, "Don't you have any good news to share? Is there any hope?" The answer is yes, there is enormous hope for all of us. The good news is coming, but we're not quite ready to hear it yet. We need to understand the depth of our problem before we can fully appreciate the wonder of God's solution.

How bad is the problem? Here is the bottom line: Sin has infected every part of your being—your mind, your emotions, your will, your intellect, your moral reasoning, your decision making, your words, and your deeds. No part of your life is exempt from the debilitating effects of sin. As someone has said, "If sin were blue, we'd be blue all over." Part would be dark blue, part would be sky blue, part would be light blue, but every part would be blue in one shade or another.

This leaves us with God's solemn statement that "there is no one righteous, not even one" (Romans 3:10). As God looks down from heaven, he doesn't see a single righteous person—not even *one*. But how can this be? How can God look down at nearly 6 billion people and not see even *one* person whose life pleases Him? Is this not an overly harsh judgment? The answer is that God judges according to a different standard from the one we use. Most of us grade on the curve. That is, we look to our neighbor and say, "I'm not as bad as he." Or we compare ourselves with someone we know at work who makes us look good, or so we think.

But God doesn't judge that way. When He looks down from heaven, the standard He uses is His own sinless perfection. He compares us to His own perfect holiness, His own perfect love, His own perfect wisdom, and His own perfect justice. Compared with God's perfection, there is no one—not even one person—who is righteous in His eyes.

LOOKING FOR A RIGHTEOUS PERSON

Where, then, will you find a righteous person on the earth? In Brazil? No. In Cambodia? No. In Japan? No. In South Africa? No. In Turkey? No. In Israel? No. In America? No. Will you find a righteous person in Congress? No. How about Hollywood? Forget it. Can you find a righteous person in the churches? Not a chance. Is there anywhere in all the earth where we could find a truly righteous man or woman? The answer is no. From God's point of view there isn't a single righteous person in the entire human race.

Let's be honest and say that even as we read these words, there is something in us that resists this harsh conclusion. When God looks down from heaven, He sees a race of people who are sinful through and through. We are like a basket of fruit that has gone rotten in the hot summer sun. We have all "gone bad" in the eyes of God.

What is the conclusion? As long as we live together on the earth there will be various races, colors, pigments, backgrounds, languages, and cultures. These differences are not evil and should not be ignored or deprecated. There is much to appreciate in the various differences in humanity. But let us be clear on this point: There is only one race in God's eyes—the human race. Secondary differences do not matter to Him the way they seem to matter so much to us.

Since we all descend from the Adam, there is no room for inordinate pride or a feeling of superiority over others. We all stand in exactly the same place— created by God, made to know Him, deeply fallen, and greatly loved. And we all need the saving touch of Jesus Christ.

Part of our problem at this point is that it's easy for us to confess someone else's sins. The tendency toward hypocrisy shows itself in many subtle ways. Have you ever noticed how we like to "rename" our sins? We do that by ascribing the worst motives to others, while using other phrases to let ourselves off the hook. If you do it, you're a liar; I merely "stretch the truth." If you do it, you're cheating; I am "bending the rules."

You lose your temper; I have righteous anger.

You're a jerk; I'm having a bad day.

You curse and swear; I let off steam.

You're pushy; I'm intensely goal oriented.

You're greedy; I'm simply taking care of business.

You're a hypochondriac; but I'm really sick.

You stink; I merely have an "earthy aroma."

And so it goes. We all have a thousand ways to excuse our own behavior while at the same time criticizing others for doing the same things. No wonder Jesus said, "Let him who is without sin cast the first stone." If we all followed that standard, the volume of criticism in the world would rapidly fall to zero.

Some time ago I talked with a good friend who is having trouble in his marriage. When I asked him what was his main problem and what was her main problem, my friend smiled ruefully and said with total honesty, "I see her problems much better than I see my own." I smiled and admitted that I'm the same way. I always look pretty good to myself. That's human nature, isn't it? All of us, even the best of us, are prone to hypocrisy because we all by nature let ourselves off the hook too easily. And when the excuse making is finally over, we come back to where we started. We are all sinners.

Your position in life doesn't change the reality of your condition before God. You may be a student

career employee

corporate executive

stay-at-home mom or dad

single parent

senior adult

man of means

woman of wealth

good citizen

It doesn't matter. You are still a sinner in the eyes of God.

THE CONSEQUENCES OF SIN

Where does all this leave us? I can sum up the biblical data this way. Because of sin we are . . .

- *Lost*—To be lost means to be in a position of great personal danger because you cannot find your way to safety.

- *Separated from God*—Sin has created a great chasm between God and us. We were made to know God, but our sin keeps us from Him. We feel it, and we know it is true. There is a thick wall between us, a mountain of sin rising up, and a deep chasm beneath us. This is why we are restless. Nothing on earth can satisfy our hunger for God.

This is why we are seeking and searching and trying and striving.

- *Blind*—Sin destroys our ability to see things clearly. We live in the darkness of sin, and not even the tiniest ray of light breaks through to us.

- *Dead*—A dead person has eyes but cannot see, ears but cannot hear, lips but cannot speak, feet but cannot move. The spiritually dead have within them no ability to respond to God. Unless someone raises them to life, they can never know the God who made them.

- *Enslaved*—Because of sin we are slaves to our own lusts. Even our hearts have been corrupted. Left to ourselves, we repeatedly choose to do wrong. Try as we might we cannot change ourselves. In the words of the cartoon character Pogo, "We have met the enemy and he is us." We are enslaved, and we cannot set ourselves free! God says, "Thou shalt not"; but we say "I shall," and then we hate ourselves afterwards. Why? We are enslaved to sin. Sin masters us, rules us, dominates us. We are a people of high ideals and weak wills, of big dreams and small deeds, of high hopes and low living.

- *Helpless*—This is the logical end of it all. A person who is lost, separated, blind, dead, and enslaved is truly helpless. He is trapped with no hope. Any help must come from somewhere else.

THE FIRST STEP IS THE HARDEST

Not long ago a man wrote to tell me about a ministry he and his wife share. Their goal is to help anyone struggling with issues of alcohol addiction. The man commented that for most alcoholics (he was speaking from personal experience), the hardest part of the process is admitting that you need help. He spoke of the difficulty of being totally honest about the mess your life is in and how easy it is to rationalize, to minimize, to make excuses, to tell part of the truth but not all the truth. Those who have been in the program will tell you that the first step is the hardest—and the most crucial. Until you face the bad news about your condition, you can't truly and totally turn your life over to God and ask for His help.

The same is true for all of us, no matter what our personal issues might be. Sin has left us powerless and enslaved, totally unable to save ourselves. Until we admit that, our lives can never really change.

It's entirely possible that you don't see your life in those terms. To say that you are a sinner doesn't mean you are as bad as you could possibly be. Few of us ever reach the lowest depths of our own sinful inclinations. But if we are honest, we must admit that even on our best days, we fall far short of God's standard of absolute perfection. Even if your life seems to be in good shape, the Bible says that you are still a sinner. This is God's verdict on the whole human race.

Here is the bottom line: You were born in sin—

separated from God, fallen, corrupt, spiritually dead. You are dying physically and dead spiritually. You are responsible for every sin you have ever committed.

You are in big trouble. Unless Someone intervenes to help you, you can never be saved.

#1 IN OPEN HEART SURGERY

I have several good friends who are undergoing very difficult chemotherapy treatments for cancer. For some it is a very unpleasant experience indeed. I know of no one who takes chemotherapy for the fun of it. You take it because the doctor says, "If you don't, you will die." So you take it as the only available remedy. If sin is the cancer of the soul, then the gospel is God's divine remedy. In fact, it is the only remedy for sin.

Recently a friend told me about a billboard posted near a Chicago freeway advertising the cardiac services of Christ Hospital in the Oak Lawn area. The billboard reads: "Christ is #1 in Open Heart Surgeries." I don't know about the hospital, but I can vouch for its namesake. Jesus Christ is indeed #1 in open heart surgery. He has never lost a case yet. When you come to Him by faith, He gives you a brand-new heart.

The gospel is good news. But until we see how bad the bad news is, we will never understand why the good news is so good.

If you are still reading this, take heart! The worst is over. Good news is just around the corner.

Chapter Three

AMAZING GRACE

In his book *What's So Amazing About Grace?* Phillip Yancey comments that grace is the "last great word." He means that it is one of the last of the old English words that has retained something of its original meaning: "free and undeserved bounty." He points out that when we pray, we "say grace" to thank God for our food. We are "grateful" for a kindness shown by another person. To show our thanks we offer a "gratuity." Something that is offered at no cost is said to be "gratis." And when we have overdue books from the library, we may return them at no charge during a "grace period."

It is commonly said that Christianity is supremely a religion of grace. And that is certainly true. We sing about grace, we write poems about grace, we name our churches and our children after grace. But for all that, grace is not well understood and often not really believed. We use the word a great deal but rarely think about what it means. Part of our problem is in the nature of grace itself. Grace is scandalous. Hard to accept. Hard to believe. Hard to receive. We all have a certain skepticism when a telemarketer tells us, "I'm not trying to sell you anything. I just want to offer you a free trip to Hawaii." Automatically we wonder, *What's the catch?* because we have all been taught that there's no free lunch.

Yancey points out that grace shocks us in what it offers. It is truly not of this world. It frightens us because of what it does for sinners. Grace teaches us that God does for others what we would never do for them. We would save the not-so-bad. God starts with prostitutes and then works downward from there. Grace is a gift that costs everything to the giver and nothing to the receiver. It is given to those who don't deserve it, barely recognize it, and hardly appreciate it.

JEFFREY DAHMER AND ME

As I pondered Yancey's words, I recalled an illustration I read not long ago. It goes something like this. Consider for a moment the deeds of Jeffrey Dahmer, the notorious serial murderer. After he was arrested and imprisoned, he professed faith in Jesus Christ. That is, he claimed to have seen the error of his ways, confessed his sins, and cried out to Jesus for forgiveness. We'll never know the full story of what happened because he was beaten to death in prison not long after that.

When we think about Jeffrey Dahmer and the possibility that he might truly have been saved after those heinous crimes, our first response may be to say, "There is grace even for people like Jeffrey Dahmer." That statement, true as it is, reveals at least as much about us as it does about him. All of us would like to think (and in fact do think) that we are "better" than Jeffrey Dahmer and that we're definitely not as bad as he was. Or we're not as "bad" as he. I make no bones about the fact that I think I am "better" than Jeffrey Dahmer. I've never done the things he did. I've never even thought or dreamed or imagined any of them. So when I say there is grace "even" for the likes of Jeffrey Dahmer, while I'm willing to include him in the circle of those God might save, I'm not putting myself on his level. I truly believe I'm better than Jeffrey Dahmer.

The man telling the story then made this comment. It's not enough to say there is grace even for the likes of Jeffrey Dahmer. In truth, there is grace *only* for the Jeffrey Dahmers of this world. They alone can be saved.

Right now you might be thinking, *This sounds crazy*. Something deep inside the human heart resists this conclusion. How can it be true? Does it mean God somehow "favors" the perverse, that grace is a reward for truly terrible sin, that the greater your sin, the more likely you are to find God's grace? That can't be right, can it?

JEFFREY DAHMER AND MOTHER TERESA

But when the smoke clears, I think there is a truth here we must consider. Too many religious people are like the Pharisee who prayed, "God, I thank you that I am not like other men—robbers, evildoers, adulterers—or even like this tax collector" (Luke 18:11). He might as well have said, "I thank God I'm not like Jeffrey Dahmer." Well, it's true. He wasn't like Jeffrey Dahmer. And he didn't experience God's grace either. He went home still in his sins, while the hated tax collector ended up justified by God.

As long as you think you are better than other people, you are not ready to be saved from your sin because you have not yet considered how great your sin really is. Jesus did not come to save "semi" sinners or "partial" sinners or "not-so-bad" sinners. As long as you feel the need to put some kind of qualifying adjective before the word *sinner*, you aren't ready to come to Jesus. You won't see your need for the grace of God.

To put the matter this way is not to deny the real moral differences among people. Is there no difference between Jeffrey Dahmer and Mother Teresa? Of course there is. One was a sadistic killer, the other an instrument of God's mercy to multitudes of hurting people. But our perspective is all-important. Let's suppose that we throw Jeffrey Dahmer into the deepest pit on earth. Then let's travel to the top of the Sears Tower in downtown Chicago. There we will look over the railing and jeer at Jeffrey Dahmer and congratulate ourselves for being so far above him. Now consider what God sees. From heaven He looks down as if the earth is a trillion miles away. What happens to the distance between us and Jeffrey Dahmer? It vanishes from God's point of view. That's why Romans 3:22 says, "There is no difference." And that's why the next verse says, "For all have sinned and fall short of the glory of God." We're all in the same boat—like it or not.

WANTED: A RIGHTEOUS MAN

I pastor a church in Oak Park, Illinois. During a sermon one Sunday, I said that there were no righteous people in Oak Park. None at all. The next Sunday, a woman shook my hand and said she wanted to ask me a question. I could tell that she was deeply concerned about something. "Last week you said there was no one righteous in all of Oak Park." That's true. I did indeed say that, and I also said there were no righteous people in any of the surrounding cities and towns. Apart from God's grace, there is no righteousness to be found anywhere. With a face marked with intense concern, she asked, "But Pastor Ray, if you aren't a righteous man, where can we find one?"

Her question was honest and sincere. I didn't say what I could have said: "If you only knew me like my family knows me, you wouldn't ask that question." Instead, I told her to listen to my sermon and she would find the answer. I recounted the story to the congregation and said I would show them the only righteous person in Oak Park—or anywhere else for that matter. Pointing to the cross on the wall behind the pulpit, I declared that Jesus is the only righteous man who ever lived.

And compared to Him, I am Jeffrey Dahmer.

Jesus Christ was pure, holy, and perfect in every way. He never sinned, not even one time. Though He was severely tempted, He never gave in. All the rest of us fall so far short that we cannot begin to be compared to Him. He is the only righteous man ever to walk this earth.

And we crucified Him. His reward for doing God's will was death on a bloody Roman cross. Here is the wonder of grace at work. From the murder of a perfect man came God's plan to rescue the human race.

This, I think, is what Phillip Yancey meant when he called grace "scandalous" and "shocking." Indeed it is. To the human heart no doctrine is more repugnant than the doctrine of grace because it forces us to admit that we are truly helpless because of our sin.

GRACE NEEDED

One of our major objections at this point involves the fact that we're not as bad we could be. We could be worse. After all, we haven't broken all of the Ten Commandments. That's certainly true for most of us, at least in the literal, outward sense. But the Bible says that to break any part of God's Law is the same as breaking all of it. In that sense, the Ten Commandments are like a ten-link chain that stretches from earth to heaven. If you break one of those links, it doesn't matter how well you keep the other nine. To break one is the same as breaking them all.

This was driven home to me when our children were young and I was watching our two younger sons while my wife went shopping with our oldest son. She hadn't been gone long when I heard a loud crash from the backyard. Before I could even get out of my chair, my youngest son ran inside and said, "Mark broke a glass in the screen door." Then before I went outside to check it, Mark came running up and said, "Don't worry, Dad. I only broke part of it." "Which part was that?" "The part down by the corner."

When I went outside to check, there was a hole about the size of my fist in the lower right-hand corner of the glass. What had happened? Well, the boys had gotten into my golf clubs and were practicing their swings. Evidently Mark's aim was not much better than mine, since he wound up and sent the ball right through the screen door. But, he assured me again, it was OK since he had broken only part of it. I patiently explained to him that it didn't work that way. If you broke any part of glass, it was as if you had broken it all, since the whole thing had to be replaced.

It's the same way with God's Law. There's no such thing as being a "moderate" sinner. That's like being a "little bit" pregnant. You're either a sinner or you're not. If you break any part of God's Law, it's as if you've broken the whole thing. You can't repair the situation by trying to make up for your sin in other areas. God won't accept that solution. It doesn't matter how good you think you are; you still stand in need of God's grace.

GRACE GIVEN

Grace means that while we were completely and totally and absolutely dead in our sins, God decided to do something to rescue us. Here are three words that describe what that "something" was—*love, mercy, and grace. Love* is God reaching out to His creatures in benevolence. *Mercy* is God withholding punishment. *Grace* is the unmerited favor of God. Think of it this way. Imagine a vast reservoir of God's love. As it begins to flow toward us, it becomes a river of mercy. As it cascades down upon us, the mercy becomes a torrent of grace.

Here's a good way to remember the difference between mercy and grace. Mercy is God not giving us what we *do* deserve—judgment. Grace is God giving us what we *don't* deserve—salvation. The picture of a mighty river of grace washing over us is especially helpful, since grace always *comes down* from God to man. Grace never goes up; it always comes down. Grace by definition means that God gives us what we don't deserve and could never earn.

GRACE RECEIVED

How is grace communicated to the human heart? The answer is simple. Grace comes to us through faith, not by works, not by religion, not by anything we

Amazing Grace | 51

might conceive as "earning" God's favor. Grace saves us through faith. Nothing more, nothing less. Something in us always wants to add to God's free grace. It's humbling to admit that we can do nothing to earn our deliverance from sin. But any time we add anything to grace, we subtract from its meaning.

Grace must be free or else it is not grace at all. Free grace? Of course. What other kind could there be?

Grace is the source, *faith* is the means, and *salvation* is the result. Or you might say that grace is the reservoir, faith is the channel, and salvation is the stream that washes my sin away. And all of it is the gift of God, even the faith that lays hold of God's grace. Even our faith is not of us. It, too, is part of God's gift. Our situation is so hopeless that salvation must come from another place. We need help that comes from outside ourselves. We are not saved by what we do but by what Jesus Christ has done for us.

We are saved by grace through faith:

> Apart from works
>
> Apart from all human "goodness"

That salvation is freely given and is received by faith alone.

"YOU AND ME, JESUS"

This view of grace is hard for good people to accept because it means we must give up our "goodness" in order to be saved. We must admit that nothing we have done matters in the least when it comes to being forgiven by God. What would heaven be like if you had to earn your way there? It would be like going to one of those $500-per-plate political dinners where people stand around bragging about how much they gave to help their candidate win the election. "I gave $5,000." "So what? I gave $10,000." "Big deal. I gave $50,000." "Move out of the way, pip-squeak. I own this guy. He's got $300,000 of my money." And so it goes.

Heaven would be just like that if you had to earn your way there. "I was chairman of the elder board." "I made tapes for blind people." "I gave a million dollars to world missions." "I helped old ladies cross the street." "I changed dressings for burn victims." As good as those things are, they will not help forgive even one sin. They will not save you or help save you.

Wouldn't it be horrible to spend eternity listening to people brag about what they did to earn their salvation? Heaven would not be heaven if that were the case. Someone would put his arm around Jesus and say, "You and me, Jesus, we did it. You died on the cross and I baked the cookies."

When Jesus died on the cross, He paid the full price for your salvation. It doesn't matter whether you baked the cookies or not. Jesus paid the price all by Himself. Entrance into heaven is limited to those who trust Jesus Christ—and Him alone—for their salvation.

ONE THOUSAND POINTS TO GO TO HEAVEN!

The following story is totally imaginary but it makes an important point. The scene: Saint Peter is manning the entrance desk by the gates of heaven. Up comes a fine-looking man, all dressed up. When he rings the bell, St. Peter says, "Can I help you?" And the man says, "I would like to have entrance into heaven." And St. Peter says, "Excellent. We're certainly glad to have you. We always want more people in heaven."

Then St. Peter says, "In order to enter heaven you have to earn a thousand points." The man says, "That shouldn't be any problem. I have been a very good man all my life. I've been very involved in civic things. I have always given a lot of money to charitable causes. For twenty-five years I was the chairman of the YMCA." As St. Peter writes it all down, he says, "That's a marvelous record. That's one point."

Taken aback, the man adds, "I was married to my wife for forty-five years. I was always faithful. We had five children—three boys and two girls. I always loved them and spent a lot of time with them and made sure they got a good education. I always took good care of them and they turned out so well. I was a real family man." St. Peter says, "I'm very impressed. We don't get too many people up here like you. That's another point."

Sweating freely by now, the man starts shaking. "You don't understand. I was active in my church. I went every Sunday. I gave money every time they passed the plate. I was a deacon and an elder. I even sang in the choir. I taught Sunday school for twenty years." And St. Peter says, "Your record is certainly admirable. That's another point." Then he adds, "Let me add this up. That's one. That's two. That's three points. Only 997 to go."

Trembling, the man falls to his knees. In desperation he cries out, "But for the grace of God nobody could get in here!" St. Peter looks at him and smiles, "Congratulations, you've just received one thousand points."

FOR SINNERS ONLY

Do you want to go to heaven? You've got to get there by the grace of God or you won't get there at all. Salvation begins when a person understands that he cannot save himself. The door to heaven has a sign over the top that reads For Sinners Only. If you qualify, you can go to heaven.

In the end, grace means that no one is too bad to be saved. Are there any truly bad people reading this chapter? I have some good news for you. God specializes in saving really bad people. Do you have some things in your background that you would be ashamed to talk about in public? Fear not. God knows all about it, and His grace is greater than your sin.

Grace also means that some people may be too "good" to be saved. That is, they may have such a high opinion of themselves that they think they don't need God's grace. They may admit they are sinners, but they won't admit they are spiritually dead. They may think they're sick because of sin but not truly dead. God's grace cannot help you until you are desperate enough to admit you need it.

The Church of the Nativity in Bethlehem is built over the reputed spot where Mary gave birth to Jesus. To get to the church, you first walk across a broad plaza and then come to a very small entrance. In fact, it's so small that you have to duck down low to get inside. The entrance is deliberately made so low because several centuries ago the local big shots liked to ride their horses right into the sanctuary. The priests felt that was inappropriate, so they lowered the entrance to force the great men to dismount before entering the church. There is a lesson here for all of us. If you want to go to heaven, you've got to get off your high horse and humble yourself before the Lord. Until you do, you'll never be saved.

That brings me to my final point. How do you find God's grace? Just ask for it. That's all. It's really that simple. The more you feel your need for grace, the better candidate you are to receive it. Hold out your empty hands and ask God for His grace. You will not be turned away.

It's never too late. Though your sins be as scarlet, God says they will be white as snow. That kind of grace is not only amazing, it's shocking and truly "out of this world." Only God would have thought of something like this.

Grace is at the heart of the good news that can change your life. And the best part is, it's free. Stay tuned for even more good news from God.

Chapter Four

A MAN
CALLED JESUS

Who is Jesus Christ? Before you answer that question, let me set the scene. It's a few minutes past noon in downtown Philadelphia. You're walking with a few friends to a favorite lunch spot when a camera crew stops you for a spontaneous interview. To your surprise, their questions have nothing to do with the White House, politics, the economy, or where you stand on capital punishment. The interviewer wants to know what you think about Jesus Christ. Who is He? While you fumble for an answer, the video camera records your discomfort. You weren't prepared for this, much less dressed for it, and now you're being quizzed on theology while your friends watch from five feet away. The seconds pass as various answers flash across your mental screen: "A good man . . . the Son of God . . . a prophet . . . a Galilean rabbi . . . a teacher of God's Law . . . the embodiment of God's love . . . a reincarnated spirit master . . . the ultimate revolutionary . . . the Messiah of Israel . . . Savior . . . a first-century wise man . . . a man just like any other man . . . King of Kings . . . a misunderstood teacher . . . Lord of the universe . . . a fool who thought he was God's Son . . . the Son of Man . . . a fabrication of the early church.

Which answer will you give? Before you answer, let me say that you can find people today who will give every one of those possible answers. But it's nothing new. When Jesus asked His disciples, "Who do people say I am?" they replied with four different answers (see Matthew 16:13–16). Even when He walked on this earth, people were confused as to His true identity. Some thought He was a prophet, others that He was a great political leader, and still others that He was John the Baptist come back to life.

One question with many answers. One man with many faces.

It's not enough to believe in Jesus. You must be certain that the Jesus you believe in is the right Jesus. In a world of spiritual counterfeits, your eternal destiny depends on knowing the Christ of God who is revealed in the New Testament.

Who is Jesus Christ? Or to borrow a phrase from television, "Will the real Jesus please stand up?" The only way to discover the real Jesus is to go to the original source—the Bible. If you would like to know Jesus personally, here are seven statements that summarize who He really is.

1. He had a supernatural entrance into the world

We know from the Old Testament that many details of His coming were predicted hundreds of years before His birth. The prophet Isaiah predicted He would be born of a virgin, and another prophet named Micah identified His birthplace as Bethlehem. The great creeds of the church use this sentence to describe His birth: "Conceived of the Holy Spirit and born of the Virgin Mary." Although we often speak of the "virgin birth," the real miracle took place nine months before Bethlehem when the Holy Spirit overshadowed Mary and created within her womb the divine-human person of the Lord Jesus Christ. The fact that He was born of a virgin means He had an earthly mother but no earthly father. No one else has ever been born in this manner.

2. He was God in human flesh

Christians use the word *Incarnation* to describe this truth. It means that when Christ was conceived in Mary, God the Son took on human flesh. Though He was God, He added humanity without subtracting from His deity. He was not half-God and half-man, but fully God and fully man, two natures united in one person. He was fully human in every respect, yet without sin. Hebrews 1:3 says that Jesus is "the radiance of God's glory and the exact representation of his being." The first phrase means that Christ is the "shining forth" of God. He is to God what sunlight is to the sun. The second phrase means that Jesus Christ bears within Himself the exact stamp of the divine nature—like a die being stamped into a piece of metal. When He was born, He was called Immanuel, "God with us." Jesus was the Son of God and God the Son. That is why when the apostle Thomas finally saw the resurrected Christ, he fell on his face and cried, "My Lord and my God!" (John 20:28).

3. He is the standard of absolute righteousness

When Jesus Christ walked on the earth, He was perfectly righteous. This speaks to two sides of His character. On the negative side, He never sinned in thought, word, or deed. He is the only "Perfect 10" who ever lived. All the rest of us have fallen far short of perfection, but not Jesus. He did not sin outwardly because He did not sin inwardly. He was without fault and without evil. He never had an evil thought, never said an evil word, never committed even one evil deed. He never cheated, never lied, never procrastinated, never got bitter, never lost His temper, never lusted, never sought an easy way out of a hard situation, never bent the truth to make Himself look good, never cursed, never turned His back on His friends, never broke any laws of God, and never deviated in the slightest degree from the path of His Father's will.

On the positive side, this means He perfectly fulfilled God's Law. He lived a life of perfect holiness, perfect purity, perfect kindness, perfect truth, and perfect goodness. Just as the first Adam sinned and all humanity fell with him, even so Christ came as the "last Adam" who through His obedience to God won salvation for all those who follow Him. He succeeded where we failed, and He obeyed where we rebelled. By His perfect life, He fulfilled everything that God required of us.

4. He did things only God can do

He made amazing claims and then backed them up with amazing deeds. He repeatedly claimed equality with God. He said that He was "one with the Father" and that to see Him was to see the Father. He spoke with divine authority: "I am the living water"; "I am the light of the world"; "I am the way, the truth, and the life." He even claimed the ability to raise Himself from the dead. People who are only vaguely familiar with Jesus tend to underestimate this part of His teaching. They like to label Him as a great moral teacher while discounting His (to them) more outlandish claims. But as C. S. Lewis remarked, a person who talked like Jesus talked, if He wasn't who He said He was, wouldn't be a good teacher. He would be a liar, or a lunatic, or the devil of hell, or something worse. You can't have Jesus without dealing with His claims of deity.

He backed up those claims by repeatedly demonstrating power over the forces of nature, sickness, and death. He even claimed the power to forgive sins.

This is what initially got Him in trouble with the Jewish leaders. They rightly saw Jesus as virtually claiming to be God, but they drew the wrong conclusion. He claimed to forgive sins because He was indeed God in human flesh.

5. He died as a sacrifice for our sins

The story of His earthly life ends this way. Though innocent of all wrongdoing, He was crucified as a common criminal. Pontius Pilate, the Roman governor, three times declared, "I find no fault in him." The Bible says He died as the just for the unjust, the innocent for the guilty, the good for the bad. He died as our substitute, standing in our place, taking our punishment, bearing our sins in His own body. With His own blood He paid the full price for our disobedience. In so doing He completely satisfied God's righteous demands and enabled God to be merciful to sinners who come to Him in Jesus' name. Through His death we are set free from the penalty of sin forever.

6. He proved His claims by rising from the dead

In many discussions with His disciples, Jesus openly predicted His death and His resurrection. Nothing that happened came as a surprise to Him. He knew it all and saw it all long in advance. Late on the evening of Good Friday, His followers tenderly took His dead body from the cross. Wrapping Him in graveclothes, they laid His corpse in a borrowed tomb not far from Skull Hill, the place where He died. On Saturday, the Romans, the Jews, and the disciples agreed on only one thing: Jesus was truly dead. Because of fears that someone might disturb the grave and remove His body, an elite squad of Roman soldiers stood guard at His tomb, which was sealed and covered with an enormous stone.

That was Saturday. Early on Sunday morning, when Mary and the other women came to the tomb, they planned to anoint His dead body. But instead they found the soldiers unconscious on the ground, the seal broken, the stone rolled away, and angels guarding the entrance. The angels announced that Jesus had risen from the dead. The women were confused and frightened and reported to the men that the tomb was empty. Later that day, and many times over the next forty days, Jesus appeared in bodily form to His disciples as well as to over five hundred other people. Then He ascended into heaven where He now sits at the Father's right hand.

After two thousand years, skeptics have never provided a sufficient answer to this question: What happened to the body of Jesus? No one ever found His dead body because by Easter Sunday it wasn't dead anymore. There is no other reasonable answer than this: Jesus Christ actually, literally, and physically rose from the dead. And from that day to this, the Christian church has made the Resurrection the cornerstone of the gospel message.

The resurrection of Jesus is vitally important because it proves that He really is the Son of God and that everything He said is true. No one else has ever come back from the dead never to die again. This means that in the most profound sense Jesus Christ is alive today. And that's why you can know Him personally. Because He is alive, He gives eternal life to those who trust in Him. And because He conquered death, those who trust in Him need not fear death, for they have assurance that they will go to heaven to be with the Lord Jesus when they die. When He returns to the earth, their bodies will be raised from the dead. All this is guaranteed to the believer because Christ rose from the dead.

7. He will one day return to the earth

With this final fact, we move from the distant past to the not-so-distant future. There is yet one more event in the "career" of Jesus Christ. One day He will return to the earth. He promised to return—"I will come again"—and He will keep that promise. He will come just as He left—visibly and bodily. His coming is not merely spiritual but actual and literal. This is truly an astounding thought. The same Jesus who was born in Bethlehem, walked on this earth, died on the cross, rose from the dead, and ascended into heaven is coming again. The actual, historical figure who lived two thousand years ago on the other side of the world is returning to the earth one more time. Though no one knows the day or the hour, the fact of His return is certain.

THE CHRIST WE NEED

Let's now wrap up this chapter with a simple

thought. Only the Christ revealed in the pages of Holy Scripture can save us. But the Jesus of the Bible is not the only "Jesus" in the marketplace of ideas. To be almost right about Jesus is to be totally wrong. Why? Because we are not saved by good opinions about Jesus. We are not saved because we have a good feeling about Jesus. We are not saved because we like His moral teaching. *We are saved by all that Jesus accomplished for us in His obedient life, His sacrificial death, and His bodily resurrection from the dead.*

A COP'S COP

I've never forgotten a police officer I met while living in California. He had been a cop's cop. He was tough with a capital T. He had seen the underside of life, and it had left him jaded and skeptical. Before he was a cop, he had served in Vietnam and had seen some horrible things. I think that's what made him live "on the edge."

He lived right across the street from the church I pastored, and his children occasionally came to Sunday school—and he and his wife would sometimes show up for a worship service. Over the months we struck up a friendship—mostly because he told the most incredible stories I had ever heard in my life. He was what you would call a "seeker." For a long time, he plied me with one question after another about the Bible and Jesus Christ, not hostile or negative but sincerely looking for the truth. He wanted to know if he could trust the Bible and if Jesus really was who He claimed to be.

One day we went to eat at a little hole-in-the-wall restaurant where they made the best tacos in town. "Let me tell you what happened to me," he said. And he proceeded to tell me that after carefully investigating all the facts, he had recently trusted Jesus Christ as Lord and Savior. "As I was reading the Bible, suddenly it hit me, 'This stuff is true!'" he declared. I will never forget his description of what happened to him: "It felt like a thousand pounds had been lifted off my shoulders."

That's what it means to encounter the real Christ of the Bible. The weight of sin is lifted off your shoulders. The guilt is gone because your sins have been forgiven.

If Jesus is who He said He is, there is no truth more worthy of your time, no person more important to know. The Christian church is made up of men and women who confess one revolutionary truth—that Jesus of Nazareth is the Son of the living God.

And until you believe that, and confess that, you cannot be called a Christian. It matters not that you may have positive feelings about Jesus Christ or that you think He was a very good man. You are not a Christian until you confess that Jesus is the Christ, the Son of the Living God.

We end this chapter where we started—with a most important question. Who is Jesus Christ? A good man? A great teacher? One of the finest fellows who ever walked the face of this earth? Or is He the Christ, the Son of the Living God?

Who is Jesus Christ? Spend a moment thinking how you would respond. Your answer determines your eternal destiny.

Chapter Five

IT IS FINISHED

Friday morning in Jerusalem. Another hot April day. Death is in the air. Word has spread to every corner of the city. The Romans plan to crucify somebody today.

A crowd gathers on the north end of town. Just outside the Damascus Gate is a place called Skull Hill. The Romans like it because the hill is beside a main road. That way lots of people can watch the crucifixions carried out there. On this day more people than usual have gathered. They come out of the morbid human fascination with the bizarre. The very horror of crucifixion draws people to Skull Hill.

This day seems like any other, but it is not. A man named Jesus is being crucified. The word spreads like wildfire. His reputation has preceded Him. No one is neutral. Some believe, many doubt, and a few hate Him.

THREE HOURS OF DARKNESS

The Crucifixion begins at nine o'clock sharp. The Romans are punctual about things like that. At first the crowd is rowdy, loud, raucous, boisterous, as if this were some kind of athletic event. They cheer, they laugh, they shout, they place wagers on how long the men being crucified will last. It appears that the man in the middle will not last long. He has already been severely beaten. In fact, it looks like four or five soldiers have taken turns working Him over. His skin hangs from his back in tatters, His face is bruised and swollen, His eyes nearly shut. Blood trickles from a dozen open wounds. He is an awful sight to behold.

There are voices from all three crosses, a kind of hoarse conversation shouted above the din. Sentence fragments float through the air. Something that sounds like "Father, forgive them," something else about "If you are the Son of God," then a promise of paradise. Finally Jesus spots His mother and speaks to her.

Then it happens. At noon "darkness falls upon all the land." It happens so suddenly that it startles everyone. One moment the sun is right overhead, the next moment it has disappeared. This is not an eclipse, nor is it a dark cloud cover. It is darkness itself, thick, inky-black darkness that falls like a shroud over the land. It is darkness without any hint of light to come. It is chilling blackness that curdles the blood and freezes the skin.

No one moves. No one speaks. For once, even the profane soldiers stop their swearing. Not a sound breaks the dark silence over Skull Hill. Something eerie is going on. It is as if some evil force has taken over the earth and is somehow breathing out the darkness. You can almost reach out and feel the evil all around. From somewhere deep in the earth there is a sound like some dark subterranean chuckle. It is the laughter of hell.

The darkness lasts for three long hours. 12:30—still dark. 1:15—still dark. 2:05—still dark. 2:55—still dark.

3:00 P.M. And just as suddenly as the darkness descended, it disappears. Voices now, and shouting. Rubbing the eyes to adjust once again to the bright sunlight. Panic on many faces, confusion on others. A man leans over to his friend and cries out, "What in God's name is going on here?"

MORTALLY WOUNDED

All eyes focus on the center cross. It is clear the end is near. Jesus is at the point of death. Whatever happened in those three hours of darkness has brought Him to death's door. His strength is nearly gone, the struggle almost over. His chest heaves with every tortured breath; His moans now are only whispers. Instinctively the crowd pushes closely to watch His last moments.

One glance at the middle cross makes clear that this man Jesus will not last much longer. He looks dead already. The soldiers know from years of experience that He won't make it to sundown.

Then it happens. He shouts something: "My God, My God, why have you forsaken me?" Someone in the crowd shouts back to Him. Moments pass, death draws near, then a hoarse whisper. "I thirst." The soldiers put some sour vinegar on a sponge, which they lift to His lips on a stalk of hyssop. He moistens His lips and takes a deep breath. If you listen, you can hear the death rattle in His throat. He has less than a minute to live.

Then He speaks again. It is a quick shout. Just one word. If you aren't paying attention, you miss it in all the confusion. He breathes out another sentence. Then He is dead.

What is that shout? "It is finished."

In the original language of the New Testament, that phrase comes from a word that means "to bring to an end, to complete, to accomplish." It's a crucial word because it signifies the successful end to a particular course of action. It's the word you would use when you reach the peak of Mt. Everest. It's the word you would use when you turn in the final copy of your term paper. It's the word you would use when you make the final payment on your new car. It's the word you would use when you cross the finish line of your first 10K run. The word means more than just "I survived." It means "I did exactly what I set out to do."

"It is finished" was the Savior's final cry of victory.

When He died, He left no unfinished business behind. When He said, "It is finished," He was speaking the truth.

PAID IN FULL

In the Greek language, the phrase *It is finished* also means *Paid in full*. Once a thing is paid for, you never have to pay for it again. That point came home to me several years ago when we visited some friends in western Colorado. When I called the husband and said we would be passing through their area, he said they would be glad to put us up. I assumed that we would be camping on sofas for the night—which was fine with us—but when I called him from southern Utah to let him know we would arrive in three or four hours, he said that he had a room for us at the local hotel—the Back Narrows Inn. I thought he was kidding. But he was serious. "Our house isn't big enough"—they had moved since we came through a few years before—"so we'll put you up in the hotel." When I protested, he said, "Don't worry about it. I've worked it out with the owner, and I've already taken care of the bill." That was that. We were staying at the hotel and he was paying. And nothing I could say would make the slightest difference.

We got to the Back Narrows Inn at about 10:00 P.M. and found it to be a small, turn-of-the-century building that had been converted into a fifteen- or twenty-room hotel. When we arrived, the owner greeted us, handed us our keys, and said, "Your friend has taken care of everything." Indeed he had. We didn't even have to formally check in. No credit cards, no filling out forms, no "How will you be paying for this, sir?" It wasn't necessary because my friend had personally paid the price in full. All that was left to us was to enjoy our rooms, provided free of charge to us by virtue of a friend's hospitality. I couldn't pay twice because my friend had already paid once. To attempt to pay on my own would be to insult my friend and to doubt that he had actually paid anything at all.

WHY JESUS HAD TO DIE

Many people hear the gospel and wonder why Jesus had to die. How could an all-knowing, all-loving God allow His Son to be murdered on a cross to redeem guilty sinners? In searching for the answer, it helps me to think of another question: Since God is both all-powerful and infinitely gracious, why didn't He simply offer forgiveness to anyone who says, "I'm sorry"? Many people secretly think that's what God should have done. Then we wouldn't have to deal with the embarrassment of God putting His own Son to death.

The solution to the dilemma goes like this. From a human point of view, God had a problem. Because God is holy, He cannot allow sin to go unpunished. His justice demands that every sin be punished—no matter how small it may seem to us. If He were to forgive sin without proper punishment, He would cease to be holy and just. God would no longer be God because He would have denied His own character. That could not happen. All offenses against God must be punished. That's why sinners can't simply say, "I'm sorry," and instantly be forgiven. Someone has to pay the price.

We often see this principle at work in the family. Through carelessness, or perhaps through deliberate disobedience, a five-year-old boy breaks an expensive lamp in the living room. Realizing what he has done, he apologizes to his father and mother, and promises never to do it again. The parents forgive their son, but the lamp is still broken. Someone has to pay for the lamp.

We follow this same principle in our criminal justice system. Suppose a man is found guilty of embezzling $700,000 from his employer. Just before sentencing, he stands before the judge, confesses his crime, begs for mercy, and promises never to embezzle money again. How would you react if the judge accepted his apology and released him with no punishment? Suppose the man had been convicted of rape and then was set free with no punishment simply because he apologized? Or what if he apologized for murdering a father and mother in front of their children—and the judge set him free? Let us go further and ask about a group of terrorists who blow up a government building, killing hundreds of people in the process. Upon their capture, trial, and conviction, they apologize and promise never to blow up a federal building again and are released on a promise of good behavior. What would we do with the judge who set them free? We would put that judge in jail and throw away the key.

Even in this life a price must be paid for breaking the law. The same is true in the spiritual realm. When sin is not punished, it doesn't seem very sinful. God's "problem" was to devise a plan of salvation whereby He would remain holy and just and still provide a way of forgiveness for guilty sinners. Somewhere, somehow, there had to be a place where grace and wrath could meet. That place is the cross of Christ.

The paradox of salvation is this: God is a God of love and therefore wants to forgive sinners. But He is also a God of holiness who must not and cannot overlook sin. How could God love sinners and yet not overlook their sin? No one would ever have dreamed of His answer. God sent His own Son to die for sinners. In that way, the just punishment for sin was fully met in the death of Christ, and sinners who trust in Christ could be freely forgiven. Only God could have done something like that.

Think of it. In the death of this one man, the price for sin has been fully paid for—past, present, and future. As a result, those who believe in Jesus find that their sins are gone forever.

This is truly good news: God's holiness demands that sin be punished. God's grace provides the sacrifice. *What God demands, He supplies.* Thus salvation is a work of God from first to last. It is *conceived* by God, *provided* by God, and *applied* by God.

NAME YOUR SIN

So let me ask you a personal question. What sin is keeping you from God right now? Is it anger? Is it lust? Is it a hard heart of unbelief? Is it alcohol abuse? Is it an uncontrollable temper? Is it cheating? Is it gambling? Is it stealing? Is it adultery? Is it abortion? Is it pride? Is it greed?

Let me tell you the best news you've ever heard. It doesn't matter what "your" sin is. It doesn't matter how many sins you've piled up in your life. It doesn't matter how guilty you think you are. It doesn't matter what you've been doing this week. It doesn't matter how bad you've been. It doesn't matter how many skeletons rattle around in your closet.

When you come to Christ, you discover that all of your sins have been stamped by God with this phrase: *Paid in full.*

Anger . . .	Paid in Full
Uncontrolled ambition . . .	Paid in Full
Gossip . . .	Paid in Full
Drunkenness . . .	Paid in Full
Fornication . . .	Paid in Full
Embezzlement . . .	Paid in Full
Lying . . .	Paid in Full
Disobedience . . .	Paid in Full
Slothfulness . . .	Paid in Full
Pride . . .	Paid in Full
Murder . . .	Paid in Full
Bribery . . .	Paid in Full

Those are just examples. Just fill in the blank with whatever sins plague your life. Through the blood of Jesus Christ, the price for "your" sins has been paid in full.

TWO SIMPLE STATEMENTS

Let me sum up what this means in two simple statements:

First, since Jesus Christ paid in full, the work of salvation is now complete. That is what Jesus' statement "It is finished" means. The debt was paid, the work was accomplished, the sacrifice was completed. And since the verb is in the perfect tense, it means that when Jesus died, He died once for all time. The sacrifice was sufficient to pay for the sins of every person who has ever lived—past, present, or future.

And that explains what Christians mean when they talk about the "finished work" of Jesus Christ. That's not just a slogan; it's a profound spiritual truth. What Jesus accomplished in His death was so awesome, so total, so complete that it could never be repeated. Not even by Jesus Himself. His work is "finished." There is nothing more God could do to save the human race. There is no Plan B. Plan A (the death of Christ) was good enough.

Second, since Jesus Christ paid in full, all efforts to add anything to what Christ did on the cross are doomed to failure. Let me put it very simply. If Jesus paid it all, you don't have to pay anything. If you try to pay for your salvation, it means you don't think He paid it all. There is no middle ground between those two propositions.

That's why going to church, keeping the Ten Commandments, increasing your education, doing good works, giving money to the poor, being baptized, moral reformation, turning over a new leaf, being a nice person, working hard at your marriage, raising model children, and trying to do your best can be such a snare. Those things, good as they are, cannot add anything to the value of what Jesus accomplished in His death on the cross. They will not help you take even one tiny step toward God. In the end it is either *all* by Jesus or not by Jesus *at all*.

God is not trying to sell you salvation. He's not offering salvation at half-price. He's not offering salvation on an installment plan. God is offering you salvation free of charge. Jesus paid in full so you wouldn't have to pay anything. Jesus left no unfinished business behind. He finished what He came to do. If you will trust Him, you will discover that in finishing His work, He paid in full the price for your sin.

Chapter Six

THE GREAT EXCHANGE

What's your credit like with God? If God is the Great Creditor, are you "in the red" or "in the black" as far as He is concerned?

That question came to mind one day as I opened my mail at home. As I sorted the envelopes into two piles, it seemed as if everything we received that day was either a credit card bill or an invitation to apply for more credit cards. Some of the invitations were quite seductive. Low interest rates, the opportunity to get "free" merchandise and special, superdiscounts on certain items that I would probably never buy at any price.

Let's take the concept of credit into the spiritual realm. How much credit do you have with God? The

Bible offers a surprising answer to that question. We are all born spiritually bankrupt and spend our lives overdrawing on an account that is already far gone "in the red." But because of what Christ accomplished on the cross, God allows bankrupt sinners who have no hope of creditworthiness, to "borrow" whatever they need based on His Son's unlimited credit in heaven. Then God pays the statement once for all! This is how we can get our lives out of spiritual debt and end up on the plus side of the ledger.

THE HEART OF THE GOSPEL

In this chapter we have finally arrived at the heart of the good news. We have already seen that when Jesus died, He paid in full for our sins. How does that apply to you and me? The answer is that God justifies wicked people who trust in Him. He credits their account in heaven with the righteousness of Jesus Christ. Thus, the guilty are acquitted on the basis of what Jesus Christ did when He died on the cross and rose from the dead.

But it is at this very point that a major problem arises. How can God acquit the guilty? Even though that is the gospel, it doesn't square with how we do things in this life. How can God acquit the guilty when on earth we put judges in jail for doing the same thing? What God does by grace, we call a miscarriage of justice. On what basis does God acquit the guilty?

WHY WORKING WON'T WORK

We begin with an astounding statement. When

God acquits the guilty, he first finds a person who isn't working for his acquittal. God looks for people who don't want to work for what they get. On the face of it, that's an incredible statement. Most of us have been raised to believe that nothing is truly free in life. You get what you work for. Work hard and you will be rewarded at the end of the day. If you don't work, you won't get ahead. True as that may be in everyday life, it's not true with regard to eternal salvation. In order for God to save you, you've got to stop working for it.

Lots of people (most people, actually) follow this motto—"We get our salvation the old-fashioned way. We earn it." But God's salvation is not a do-it-yourself kit. If you want to go to heaven, the first step is to stop trying to earn your way there. You have to "stop working" and "start trusting" if you want to be saved. Write it in big letters. When it comes to saving your soul, WORKS DON'T WORK!

WHAT GOD WANTS FROM US

If God doesn't want our "works," what does He want from us? He wants us to trust Him. That's all. Nothing more, nothing less, nothing else. In the New Testament, the terms *faith*, *trust*, and *belief* all come from the same general root word meaning "to lean wholly upon," as when you lie down on a bed, resting your whole weight upon it. We are to trust God so completely that we take Him at His Word regarding our salvation.

One crucial distinction must be made. To say that

we must trust God does not mean that our faith is something we ourselves do. Faith is not a work that "merits" salvation. Faith is the *condition*, not the *ground* of salvation. Faith cannot save us unless our faith is based upon the person and work of the Lord Jesus Christ, who died for our sins.

What is faith? Faith is the hinge that joins the sinner to God. Faith looks to the Cross and says, "Jesus Christ died for me." Faith cries out to God, "Be merciful to me, a sinner, for Jesus' sake." And God hears that prayer every time.

"NOT GUILTY!"

The word *justify* means to declare righteous. It is a legal term that refers to the final verdict by which a judge declares that an accused person is "not guilty" and is "innocent" of all charges. Applied to the spiritual realm, it means that God declares the believing sinner righteous on the basis of the death and resurrection of Jesus Christ. Since Christ paid the penalty for the sinner, the sinner is now righteous in the eyes of the Lord. Though he himself is truly guilty, through faith he receives the benefit of Christ's death on his behalf. Jesus paid the penalty, and the sinner goes free. If you are justified, it means that in the record book by your name there are no marks against you. It means the charges are dropped. There is no guilt, no penalty, no condemnation. Every demand of the Law has been met in full.

The Bible says that God justifies the wicked. This is hard for many people to accept. Many people think

God wants good people in heaven, so they spend their lives trying to be good enough to go there when they die. Wrong! No one can ever be good enough to go to heaven. So many of us are mixed up on this point. We think God is saying, "Clean up your act and then I'll save you." Or we think God is saying, "I'll clean up your act and then I'll save you." God never says any such thing. He says something entirely different: "I'll save you while you are still dirty, and then I'll help you clean up your act." Mark it down. God saves the ungodly while they are still ungodly. That's the miracle of justification. And when you come to Christ—still dirty and unclean—not only does He save you, but He begins an inner process of cleansing that changes you from the inside out. But He saves you first; then He cleans you up.

Many people don't come to Christ because they feel they aren't good enough. They feel as if they are lost in sexual sin, lost in addiction to alcohol and drugs, trapped in anger or bitterness, chained forever to a terrible, destructive way of life. But God is not in the business of justifying the good. He is in the business of justifying the bad. He doesn't justify the righteous. He justifies the wicked while they are still wicked.

The verdict is just in from heaven, and the bad news is, *you are guilty*. The good news is, *Christ is entirely righteous*. If you will accept those two rulings from the court of heaven, an amazing miracle will take place. Christ will take your guilt and exchange it with His righteousness.

Here is where the glory of the gospel is clearly seen. *It provides for us what we could never provide for ourselves.* On our own merits, we all stand condemned before the Almighty. Who would dare to say, "I am good enough to go to heaven"? As someone has said, "A clear conscience is the result of a poor memory." The only people who think they are good enough to go to heaven are the people who don't know how bad they really are. Righteousness is what we need but do not have. Therefore, God, knowing that we could never be righteous on our own, has provided a righteousness which comes down to us from heaven above. It's not earned or deserved, but is given to us by God as a free gift.

DO VS. DONE

In this we see the simplicity of Christianity when compared with the religions of the world. Religion is spelled with two letters: D-O. Religion is a list of things people think they have to *do* in order to be accepted by God—go to church, give money, keep the Ten Commandments, be baptized, pray every day, and do good works. The list is endless. It's always Do . . . Do . . . Do. If you want to go to heaven, you're going to *do* something and keep on doing it until the day you die.

Christianity is spelled with four letters—D-O-N-E. Christianity is not based on what we *do* but upon what Jesus Christ has already *done*. If you want to go to heaven, you don't have to *do* anything; you just have to trust in what Jesus Christ has already *done* for you.

That's the whole difference—*Do* versus *Done*. Either you *do* it yourself or you believe that Jesus Christ has already *done* it for you.

A TALE OF THREE SOCKS

Perhaps an illustration will help. Let's begin with three socks—one blue, one red, and one white. The blue sock represents your sin, the red sock represents the blood of Christ, and the white sock represents the righteousness of Christ. Take the blue sock and put it over your right hand. That represents your sin. It covers you so completely that you are a sinner through and through. If you attempt to come into God's presence with your sin exposed, you will be judged and sent to hell. Now put the red sock over the blue one so that it covers the blue (sin) completely. That represents the covering of your sin with the blood of Christ. Then put the white sock over the red one, which is how God sees you in Christ. The white covers the red that covers the blue. Once your sins are covered with the blood, God credits you with the righteousness of His Son, the Lord Jesus Christ. That's the miracle of the gospel.

SWAPPING GRADES WITH JESUS

But that's only part of the story. Let's further suppose that I have obtained a copy of your transcript with your "official" grades. No, not your high school grades. I'm thinking of something more serious than that. Somehow I have gotten a copy of your "permanent record" from the "Principal's Office" in heaven.

Unfortunately, the news is not good. Your grade in every course is the same:

> Seeking God — F
>
> Doing Good — F
>
> Obeying God — F
>
> Keeping the Law — F
>
> Being Perfect — F

Not a pretty picture. How would you like it if we changed your grades? I've got some good news to share with you. The valedictorian of the class is quite willing to switch grades. His name is Jesus Christ, and He made an A in each class. Here is your final grade from God:

> God's Honor Roll — A

The lesson is simple. If God gave you a report card on your life without Jesus Christ, it would be covered with black marks for all the sins you have committed. Indeed, God gives you and the whole human race an F. You flunk every test. But when you come to Jesus, your F is washed away and your sins are gone forever.

What grade would God give you? You get the grade Christ earned because He finished His course at the top of the class. You don't squeak by with God. You make the honor roll. You go to the head of the class. Why? Because you are so good? No. Left to yourself you would still flunk every course. If you have trusted Jesus Christ, you get an A because you are united with Him.

The same righteousness that once required that you get an F now requires that you get an A. You are not half-justified and half-condemned. You are not partially forgiven and partially punished. You are altogether forgiven. Your record is wiped clean. You are declared righteous in the eyes of God. That's what justification is all about.

THE TEXAS BILLIONAIRE

Let's put both sides of the truth together with one final illustration. We begin by supposing that somehow you owe the bank a million dollars. You promise that you will pay back your debt at the rate of $10 per week. On a given day you come to the bank, ready to make your $10 payment. When you hand over the $10 bill, the teller checks your account and says, "According to our records, you don't owe any money at all. In fact, someone has paid your debt and deposited a million dollars in your account."

For a moment you say nothing, stunned by your sudden good fortune. Who could have done such a thing? Who would have the money to pay the million dollars you owe plus put a million dollars extra into your account? The answer comes as a man steps out of the shadows. From articles you've read, you recognize him as a billionaire from Texas. "I paid your debt," he says, "and then I decided to give you a little spending money besides." "Sir, you shouldn't have. I'll try to pay you back someday," you reply. To which the answer comes, "Don't worry. I'm a billionaire ten times over. I've got so much money, I don't know how to spend it all. Don't even think about paying it back. It's a gift."

Could such a thing happen? Yes—at least in my dreams. The billionaire from Texas truly does have enough money to do that. In fact, he's got enough money to do that for perhaps five thousand different people. But eventually even he would run out of money.

Not so with Jesus Christ. The Texas billionaire is a pauper compared to Him. He can forgive all your sins and give you His perfect righteousness. And He can do the same thing for every other person in the world who comes to Him by faith because His righteousness is infinite and His blood never loses its power.

God has a simple proposition for you. If you admit you are a sinner, He offers to declare you righteous. All you have to do is lay hold of Jesus. Trust in Him and your sins will be forgiven, your record in heaven will be wiped clean, and you will be declared righteous in the eyes of God.

Have you ever believed what God has said about His Son, the Lord Jesus Christ?

—He is the Savior of the world and the only way to God.

—He came from heaven for you.

—He died on the cross, paying the price for your sins.

—He rose from the dead on the third day.

—He is ready to forgive you.

—He wants to give you His perfect righteousness.

Have you ever said, "Yes, Lord, I believe those things to be true"? When you get to heaven, you will discover that God is as good as His Word. In the end, it is your faith in Jesus Christ—not your works—that God counts as righteousness.

Chapter Seven

WHAT IS SAVING FAITH?

The question posed by the title of this chapter is not as easily answered as one might assume. It is evident from reading the New Testament that not everyone who "believes" truly possesses saving faith. Jesus Himself warned in Matthew 7:21–23 (NASB) that on the Day of Judgment many will claim to have worked miracles in His name, but He will say to them, "I never knew you; depart from Me." And James 2:19 informs us that even the demons believe in God—and tremble because of that belief. Yet they are not saved.

On the other hand when a man asked, "What must I do to be saved?" this simple reply was given, "Believe in the Lord Jesus, and you will be saved"

(Acts 16:31). That's clear, isn't it? Believe and be saved. A multitude of verses (especially from the gospel of John) could be added that say the same thing. The problem is not with the words but with their meaning.

That raises a key question. If salvation is based on believing in Christ, how do you know when you have truly believed? We all understand that the word *believe* has many different nuances. For instance, if I say, "I believe it's going to rain tomorrow," that's nothing more than a hunch. Or if I say, "I believe George Washington was the first President of the United States," that refers to a settled historical fact. But if I say, "I believe in Jesus with all my heart," I have made a different sort of statement altogether.

THREE ELEMENTS OF SAVING FAITH

True saving faith involves the intellect, the emotions, and the will. The faith that saves us involves all that we are in coming to Christ. Faith starts with *knowledge*, moves to *conviction*, and ends with *commitment*. Let's briefly take a look at each element.

1. Knowledge

Knowledge refers to the factual basis of the Christian faith. It speaks of intellectual understanding of the truth. You must know something in order to be saved. Faith is based on knowledge, and knowledge is based on truth. Truth must be proclaimed before saving faith can be exercised. Saving faith is intelligent faith. The right believing of right knowledge is

necessary for salvation. The gospel is about informa
tion that we need to know. You aren't saved by infor
mation, but you can't be saved without it.

Suppose you are in a burning building and cannot find your way out. "Where is the exit?" you cry.
Through the smoke and haze comes the answer:
"Go down the hallway, turn left, go down one flight
of stairs. The exit is on the right." Are you saved because you know where the exit is? No, you still have
to make the journey yourself. But if you don't know
how to get there, or if you have wrong information,
you're going to burn to death. You aren't saved by
knowing the truth, but you can't be saved without
it.

We must be perfectly clear on this point. Christian faith is not blind faith. We are called to believe
in something—not just anything. True saving faith
rests first and foremost in Jesus Christ. This is para-
mount. We must know who He is, why He came,
why He died, why He rose from the dead, and how
He can be our Lord and Savior. I am not suggesting
that we must pass a theology exam in order to be
saved, but we must know something about these
truths if our faith is to rest on the right foundation.
Faith must be grounded in the facts of divine revelation. Faith rests on facts, not on thin air. Faith in the
wrong thing, however sincere, will not save anyone.

Knowledge is essential, but it alone can never save
you. Saving faith begins with knowledge, but it never ends there.

2. Conviction

Conviction means to know something and then to be persuaded that it is true. The most common word in the Bible for "believe" means "to have confidence in, to regard as completely reliable." That Hebrew word comes over into English as "Amen," which literally means "Yes, it is true." Saving faith involves saying "Amen" to the facts of the gospel.

A man may go to a doctor who tells him he has cancer. "But there is good news," says the doctor. "We have just discovered a chemotherapy that can cure your cancer. Do you believe it?" "Yes," you answer. Are you cured? No, not until you roll up your sleeve and let them stick in the needle and pump the lifesaving medicine into your veins.

Conviction is essential because you must be personally convinced of the truth, but that alone cannot save you. There is one final element in true saving faith.

3. Commitment

Commitment speaks to the active part of faith. We might use the word *trust* in the sense of "relying fully upon," such as resting with your full weight on a bed, confident that it can hold you up. True faith always reaches out to rest upon some object. If we go to a doctor, we must rest our faith in him. If we go to a lawyer, we must put our case in his hands. This is what is meant by phrases such as *believe in your heart or believe with your heart*. It means to "embrace" or to "accept" or to "receive" or to "welcome" someone or something.

True saving faith always ends in personal commitment. Sales people understand this principle. After the presentation is made, at some point customers have to sign on the dotted line. If they say, "I know that's a good product," you haven't made a sale. If they say, "I believe I need that," they are closer but you still haven't made a sale. But when they say, "Where do I sign?" you've just closed the deal.

THE GREAT BLONDIN

In the nineteenth century the greatest tightrope walker in the world was a man named Charles Blondin. On June 30, 1859, he became the first man in history to walk on a tightrope across Niagara Falls. Over twenty-five thousand people gathered to watch him walk 1,100 feet suspended on a tiny rope 160 feet above the raging waters. He worked without a net or safety harness of any kind. The slightest slip would prove fatal. When he safely reached the Canadian side, the crowd burst into a mighty roar.

In the days that followed, he would walk across the Falls many times. Once he walked across on stilts; another time he took a chair and a stove with him and sat down midway across, cooked an omelet, and ate it. Once he carried his manager across riding piggyback. And once he pushed a wheelbarrow across loaded with 350 pounds of cement. On one occasion he asked the cheering spectators if they thought he could push a man across sitting in a wheelbarrow. A mighty roar of approval rose from the crowd. Spying a man cheering loudly, he asked, "Sir, do you think I could safely carry you across in this wheelbarrow?" "Yes, of course." "Get in," the Great Blondin replied with a smile. The man refused.

That makes it clear, doesn't it? It's one thing to believe a man can walk across by himself. It's another thing to believe he could safely carry you across. But it's something else entirely to get into the wheelbarrow yourself. That's the difference between knowledge, conviction, and commitment.

"THAT'S AMAZING!"

If you know what it means to believe a doctor when he says, "You need surgery," you know what it means to have faith. If you know what it means to step into an airplane entrusting your safety to the captain in the cockpit, you know what it means to have faith. If you know what it means to ask a lawyer to plead your case in court, you know what it means to have faith. Faith is total reliance upon another person to do that which you could never do for yourself.

How much faith does it take to go to heaven? It depends. The answer is not much and all you've got. If you are willing to trust Jesus Christ with as much faith as you happen to have, you can be saved. But if you're holding anything back, thinking that maybe you need to do something to help save yourself, forget it! True saving faith expresses itself by reaching out to take Christ as our Savior and Lord—and not before then.

—It may be expressed through a prayer of personal trust in Christ.

—It may be expressed through baptism.

—It may be expressed through a "public profession."

But those things alone are not saving faith. Saving faith understands the gospel, believes the gospel, and then commits to the gospel as the only hope of salvation. Saving faith reaches out and trusts Christ as Lord and Savior.

While serving as a guest host on a national call-in program called *Open Line*, I took a call from a young girl named Angela, who asked how you can know you are saved. I quoted 1 John 5:13, which says that you can know that you have eternal life through believing in Christ. I told Angela that salvation depends on trusting Jesus Christ. It's more than just believing facts about Jesus. To trust in Christ means to rely completely upon Him. You trust the airline pilot to get you back down on the ground safely. You trust your doctor when you take the medicine he prescribes. You trust your lawyer when you let him represent you in court. God says that when you trust Jesus Christ in that same way you are saved from your sins. All you have to do is trust Christ completely, and you can be saved. When I asked Angela what she thought about that, she blurted out, "Wow! That's amazing." Yes it is. It's the most amazing truth I know.

WHAT ABOUT REPENTANCE?

At this point someone may ask where repentance fits into the gospel message. After all, the very first word Jesus spoke in his public ministry was the word *repent*. The word *repentance* literally means "to change the mind." It has to do with the way you think about something. You've been thinking one way, but now you think differently. That's repentance—the changing of the mind.

Let's suppose a man wants to learn how to parachute. So he goes to a skydiving school and they show him how to rig up his gear, how to pull the rip cord, and how to land safely. Finally the day comes when they take him up in an airplane. He's scared to death, but he's afraid to back out. The moment comes when he is to jump. He goes to the door of the airplane and sees the ground seven thousand feet below. His legs grow weak, he's getting sick, and somebody behind him is trying to push him out of the airplane. At the last second he says, "No. I'm not going to do it." "Go ahead, you can do it," his instructor shouts. "I've changed my mind," he replies. "I'm not going to jump." And he doesn't. That man has repented. He's changed his mind in a decisive way.

That story illustrates how repentance works. Repentance is a change in the way you think that leads to a change in the way you live. When you really change your mind about something, it's going to change the way you think about it, talk about it, feel about it, and ultimately what you do about it.

True repentance and saving faith go together. They are like two sides of the same coin. To *repent* means to change your mind about whatever is keeping you from coming to Christ. To *trust Christ* means to wholeheartedly reach out to Him by faith so that He becomes your Savior and Lord.

THE POWER OF FEEBLE FAITH

One day a woman with a serious bleeding problem came to Jesus as He passed along a narrow, crowded street. She reached out, touched the corner of His cloak, and was instantly healed. After twelve years of misery, just one touch and her disease was gone forever. This story is helpful because the woman never said anything to Jesus. No doubt she was both afraid and ashamed to address Him openly. Even after her miraculous healing, she didn't say a word. She simply found him in the crowd, touched His cloak, was wonderfully healed, and then turned to go. Only at that point did Jesus address her. "Your faith has made you well; go in peace" (Luke 8:48 NASB).

In this poor woman, we see the amazing power of feeble faith. She knew who Jesus was (that's knowledge), she believed He could help her (that's conviction), and she reached out and touched Him in the crowd (that's commitment). She didn't have a huge amount of faith. But she had a tiny grain of faith, and through it, God moved the mountain of her illness.

How simple it is to come to Christ. Only a touch and this woman was healed. Not by her toiling, not by her promises to do better, not by an offer to do something for Jesus if He would do something for her. No deals here. She reached out a trembling hand and, in an instant, she was healed. It wasn't even a long process. It happened so fast that it could only be called a miracle.

That's what feeble faith can do. Coming to Christ is not difficult. The hardest part is reaching out with the hand of faith. If you want to touch Jesus, all you have to do is reach out to Him.

That's the power of feeble faith when it is directed toward the right object. You don't have to have strong faith. You can have weak faith as long as it is resting upon a strong object. And who could be stronger than Jesus Christ Himself?

Do you ever feel as if your problems keep you from coming to God? Do you ever feel so dirty and unclean that you think Jesus would not have anything to do with you? Do not despair. Jesus is not offended by your problems. He's seen it all before. He will not turn you away.

CHRIST STANDING AT THE DOOR

In the last book of the Bible, we find the image of Christ standing at the door and knocking. The picture comes from Revelation 3:20, where Christ offers to enter a lukewarm, lethargic church and have fellowship with those who will let Him in. It is a wonderful picture of how Christ comes to each of us.

And in this picture we see the three elements of faith made clear.

> I hear the knock — That's knowledge
>
> I go to the door — That's conviction
>
> I open the door — That's commitment

Only then does Christ come and make Himself at home in my heart. Years ago I learned a children's chorus that goes like this: "One door and only one, and yet its sides are two. Inside and outside, on which side are you?"

This is a crucial question for all of us to consider. On which side of your heart's door is Jesus Christ? Is He on the inside, or is He on the outside, still knocking, waiting for you to open the door? If you hear Christ knocking, do not delay. Go to the door and let Him in. This is true saving faith.

Chapter Eight
COMING TO CHRIST

If you've read this far, you probably know what comes next. It's time to talk about opening the door and welcoming Christ into your life as Savior and Lord. Before we do that, however, I'd like to share an unusual story of how one man came to Christ. It all started when Bob Johnsen introduced me to his brother Jim. When I met him, Jim was desperately sick with cancer that had returned after some years of remission. Jim could not stand because the pain was so great. We shook hands and he asked me in a desperate voice if I would pray for him. He sounded like a man in need of a Savior but who didn't know where to look. For a month or two I shook his hand each time I saw him in church and tried to encourage him as best I could.

One day Bob called and said that Jim had been taken to the hospital and wanted to see me. When I entered the room, he said, "Pastor, I've got a lot of things I want to tell you." And he slowly unfolded his life story. He told me that as a child he had been raised in a Christian family yet for many years had been away from the Lord. He had spent a long time in the military and was very proud of his service, but during those years he had drifted away from God. Some years ago he had contracted cancer. He had been treated and the cancer had gone into remission. But now it had returned in force. "I'm a dead man," he said. "The doctors won't say it, but I know the truth. The cancer is in the spine. I doubt I'll ever get out of the hospital."

He spoke of his years of wandering like the "forty days and forty nights" when the rain came down before the great flood of Noah's day. Something had clearly happened in his life recently, but I didn't know what. Then he told me that one day he heard the familiar children's song: "Jesus Loves Me" and began to sing along. In his own words, as he sang, "it happened." What happened? He trusted Jesus Christ while singing "Jesus loves me," and had a definite conversion experience. It was real, it was clear, it was a powerful change in his life.

As he told me the story, at one point he grabbed my lapel and said, "Pastor Ray, you've got to tell the young. Tell them that Christ is the only answer. The young people need to know this so they won't waste as many years as I did." He then asked me to share his story with everyone I could. "I want to help as many people as I can while I'm still alive."

Then he said something I didn't expect. "I know I'm going to heaven, but there's only one problem. I don't have a certificate." I had no idea what he meant. Evidently some of his friends had said that he needed a certificate to be sure he was going to heaven—perhaps some sort of church membership or baptismal certificate. Whatever the meaning, this troubled him greatly because he had nothing to show to others. Four times he said with great emotion, "But I don't have a certificate." I could tell the matter troubled him greatly.

After I got back to the church, I decided that if Jim needed a certificate, we could give him one. So I wrote down some things and gave it to my secretary. She designed a nice certificate that we printed on a paper with a nice border. After it was signed, we put it in a frame. It said something like this:

Upon the testimony of God's Word
and upon his profession of faith in Jesus Christ

Jim Johnsen

is a born-again Christian
who has trusted in Jesus Christ as His Lord and Savior.
"He who has the Son has life;
he who does not have the Son of God does not have life."
1 John 5:12

"Jesus loves me, this I know, for the Bible tells me so."

When I gave him the certificate, he wept for forty-five minutes. Later his family placed the certificate on the wall where he could see it. During his last days, he showed the certificate to everyone who visited him. After the funeral, we placed the certificate in the coffin, where it will be with his body until the day of the Resurrection.

That story illustrates many things, not least that there is hope for all of us. It also tells us that coming to Christ is a matter of the heart reaching out in faith to the Lord, not simply reciting some words or going through a religious ritual. Jim Johnsen found out that it's never too late to come to Christ. And you don't need a certificate to be certain that you will go to heaven when you die. The few words we wrote on that piece of paper simply summarized the message of this book. You don't need a certificate to go to heaven, but you do need to put your trust in Jesus Christ and Him alone.

The gospel is God's answer for those who aren't ashamed to admit they need help. If that is true, why do some people wait so long to come to Jesus? One man told me that many people wait because "they haven't hit bottom yet." Certainly many people feel self-sufficient and think they don't need the Lord. One can only pray that when they do hit bottom, they will finally look up and cry out for help. Procrastination keeps many people from God. We always think there is more time to decide. But life is so uncertain. One moment you are on top of the world; the next moment your plane crashes and your earthly life is over.

There comes a time when you must decide where you stand with Jesus. No one can sit on the fence forever. Not to decide is a decision in itself. If you don't say yes to Christ, you are actually saying no. To borrow a phrase from Billy Graham, there is an "hour of decision" that comes to all of us sooner or later. I pray that this might be your hour to say yes to Jesus Christ.

THE GOSPEL MADE PLAIN

Since we are near the end of this book, let's take a moment to review what we've learned so far. I can summarize the whole gospel message in seven simple statements:

> Admitting my need: To know the God who made me
>
> Accepting God's judgment: Guilty as charged
>
> Facing the truth: Helpless to save myself
>
> Acknowledging God's solution: The Lord Jesus Christ
>
> Remembering what He did: The Cross and the empty tomb
>
> Transferring your trust: From self to Christ alone

Receiving eternal salvation: His righteousness
for my sin

If you understand what those phrases mean, you
know everything you need to know to go to heaven.
The gospel begins with the God who made us. Although we were made to know Him, sin has separated
us from Him. Because of sin we are truly guilty in
God's eyes and left in a helpless condition, unable to
save ourselves. Apart from divine grace we will die in
our sins. If God doesn't do something, we're lost forever. The good news of the gospel is that God did
something. He sent His Son, the Lord Jesus Christ,
who perfectly fulfilled God's will and perfectly
obeyed God's Law. He succeeded where all of us
failed so miserably. When He died, He died not for
Himself (for He was sinless), but in our place, as a
condemned man, bearing our sin and taking our punishment. What we deserved He took in our place. He
made good on all His claims by rising from the dead
on the third day. Salvation is offered to one and all
on the condition that we turn from self-trust and self-
confidence to trust wholly and completely in Christ
alone. When we trust Christ in that fashion, God
credits the righteousness of Christ to us, and the
penalty for our sin is paid in full. Thus we receive the
benefit of what Christ accomplished two thousand
years ago. This is the gospel of Jesus Christ.

The Bible uses a number of words and phrases to
describe what happens to us when we wholeheartedly trust in Christ as Lord and Savior. We are forgiven,

saved, born-again, declared righteous in God's sight, given new life, pardoned, set free from the penalty of sin, brought into a new relationship with God, called a child of God, and assured of going to heaven when we die. This is "total salvation." It's free to us, but it's not cheap. It cost God the death of His one-and-only Son.

All of this is available to anyone and everyone who wants it. God's offer is now on the table. What will you do with it?

SALVATION MADE SIMPLE

A friend sent me an E-mail telling about a question asked by a co-worker:

> How is a Christian defined? It used to be that if you were not Jewish or Hindu or Buddhist, you were a Christian, whether Catholic or Lutheran or Episcopal or Baptist. But it seems now that the word means something more specific. Is it considered to be an actual religion other than Catholic or Lutheran or Episcopal or Baptist or whatever. If so, what makes it different?

That's a very good question. It shows that the person has been doing some serious thinking about spiritual issues. It also reveals that she has penetrated to a core issue that has long confused millions of people: What is the difference between being a Christian and a church member? The simplest way to answer that question is to say that a Christian is a person who has come to know God deeply and personally through a genuine saving faith in the Lord Jesus Christ. To say it that way means that while nearly all Christians are church members, not all church members are necessarily true Christians. Knowing God through Christ is about a personal relationship made possible through faith; it is not about religious ritual or merely "joining a church."

That truth leads us to an important point: No one "drifts" into Christianity by accident. At some point you must consciously trust Christ as Lord and Savior. In the words of Charles Spurgeon, "You will never go to heaven in a crowd." It's true there will be crowds in heaven, but we only go there one at a time. God saves individuals, not masses or groups.

John 1:12–13 offers a simple outline of what it means to come to Christ for salvation: "Yet to all who received him, to those who believed in his name, he gave the right to become children of God—children born not of natural descent, nor of human decision or a husband's will, but born of God."

A SIMPLE STEP—RECEIVING HIM

"To all who received him." The way of salvation begins with a simple step: Receiving Christ as Lord and Savior. The word *receive* means to welcome a visitor into your home. It's what happens when someone knocks at your door and you open the door and invite them to come in. To receive Christ means to welcome Him as an honored guest and to have Him make your heart His home.

A WONDERFUL RESULT—CHILD OF GOD

"He gave the right to become children of God." The word *right* means "honor" or "privilege." The moment you receive Christ into your life, God gives you the honor of becoming a member of His family. This teaches us that not everyone is a child of God. All are created by God, but not everyone in the world is a child of God. Sometimes people carelessly say, "We're all God's children," but the Bible says no such thing. God only gives the privilege of being His children to those who by personal faith receive Jesus as Lord and Savior.

That leads to some questions you ought to ask yourself:

"Not everyone is a child of God. Am I?"

"Not everyone has eternal life. Do I?"

"Not everyone will go to heaven. Will I?"

A MYSTERIOUS TRUTH—BORN OF GOD

"Children born not of natural descent, nor of human decision or a husband's will, but born of God." (John 1:13). This verse teaches us that God's grace doesn't run automatically from one generation to another. You aren't a Christian just because your parents were Christians or because your grandfather was an Episcopal bishop or your uncle a Baptist deacon. And you won't get brownie points with God just because you come from a good family and have a fine education. You can't save yourself by human effort, so don't bother

trying. The sooner you stop trying to save yourself, the sooner you can be saved by God.

The whole gospel is contained in the little phrase *born of God*. Salvation is of the Lord. It's a free gift—totally free and totally of grace. It's not a cooperative venture where you do your part and God does His. But someone may object, "Don't I have a part to play in salvation?" You do indeed have a part. Your part is to be hopelessly lost in sin. God's part is to save you. That way God alone gets the credit. Salvation is a work of God from first to last.

THREE FROGS ON A LOG

That brings us at last to the moment of decision. Before we come to the bottom line, I'd like to stop and pose a simple question. It goes like this. Three frogs are sitting on a log. Two decide to jump off. How many are left? That's not a hard question. Three minus two equals one. But one is not the right answer. The right answer is three. You haven't jumped off the log because you decided to jump. The frog is still on the log until he actually jumps off. Until then you're just "making a decision."

Sometimes we describe people who can't make a decision as being "on the fence." That perfectly describes the way many people relate to Jesus Christ. They want to know Him, they know they need Him, they truly feel their sin and want to find forgiveness, and perhaps they've even "decided to jump." But until they jump, they are still on the fence regarding Jesus. To use a biblical term, they are still lost.

To decide to receive Christ is good. Receiving Him by faith is much better.

Two thousand years ago Pontius Pilate asked the crowd, "What do you want me to do with Jesus?" "Crucify him!" they cried out. He asked the question because he wanted to shift responsibility for the decision away from himself. That never works. In the end each of us must decide what we will personally do with Jesus.

Curiosity is good if it leads you to the truth. Endless argument can be a way of avoiding the truth. In the end truth demands a personal commitment. You can talk about it, discuss it, debate it, and dissect it, but eventually you've got to do something about it. From God's point of view, believing in Christ is both an invitation and a command. In light of all that Christ has done, we are invited to trust Him as Lord and Savior. But this is not merely an option we can take or leave as if we might find a better offer somewhere else. To say that God commands us to believe in Christ means that if we refuse His offer of eternal life we will regret our wrong decision for all eternity. According to the Bible, the sin of unbelief is the greatest of all sins. Those who do not believe in Jesus are under God's wrath already. This solemn truth should make us stop and think carefully. Great issues are at stake. We must not trifle with the gospel.

The Old Testament contains a fascinating story about fiery serpents sent by God to the people of Israel as a judgment on their sin. When the people cried out for mercy, God told Moses to affix a bronze snake to a pole and place it where all the people could see it. Then they were told to look at the serpent on the pole, and they would be spared. Look and live. Such a simple action, yet with such enormous consequences. The New Testament applies that story to the work of Jesus Christ. Just as the bronze serpent was lifted up in the wilderness, even so Jesus was "lifted up" on the cross to die for our sins. The invitation from God is the same. Look and live! Look in faith to Jesus and you will have eternal life. If you refuse to look, you will die. If you look, you will live.

RISKING ETERNITY ON JESUS

Ponder the words of this little verse:

> Upon a life I did not live,
>
> Upon a death I did not die,
>
> I risk my whole eternity.

That is what it means to be a Christian. It means trusting in Christ so much that you risk your eternity on what He did for you in His life and in His death. I have sometimes told people that trusting Jesus for salvation means to trust Him so completely that if He can't take you to heaven, you aren't going to go there. Are you willing and ready to do that?

Perhaps it will help you to form your words into a very simple prayer. Even while I encourage you to pray this prayer, I caution you that saying words alone will not save you. Prayer doesn't save. Only

Christ can save. But prayer can be a means of reaching out to the Lord in true saving faith. If you pray these words in faith, Christ will save you. You can be sure of that.

> *Lord Jesus, for too long I've kept You out of my life. I know that I am a sinner and that I cannot save myself. No longer will I close the door when I hear You knocking. By faith I gratefully receive Your gift of salvation. I am ready to trust You as my Lord and Savior. Thank You, Lord Jesus, for coming to earth. I believe You are the Son of God who died on the cross for my sins and rose from the dead on the third day. Thank You for bearing my sins and giving me the gift of eternal life. I believe Your words are true. Come into my heart, Lord Jesus, and be my Savior. Amen.*

If you have prayed this prayer in sincere faith, you may want to put your initials by the prayer along with today's date as a reminder that you have come to Christ in faith, trusting Him as your Lord and Savior.

In the end, I can't believe for you or you for me. Jesus said, "Come unto me." Will you come? Come and see for yourself. Come and discover how Christ can change your life.

If you are fearful, put your heart at ease. He avoids no seeker. He will not turn you away. You will see for yourself. God invites you. But still you must come. Do not hesitate. Stop making excuses. Come to Christ and be saved. Trust in Him and your new life will begin.

JUST AS I AM

In 1822 a young woman named Charlotte Elliott was visiting some friends in the West End of London and there met a noted minister named César Malan. Over supper he asked her if she was a Christian. When she replied that she did not want to talk about the subject, the minister replied, "I did not mean to offend you. But I want you to know that Jesus can save you if you will turn to Him." Several weeks later they met again and Miss Elliott said that she had been trying to come to Christ but did not know how to do it. "Just come to Him as you are," Dr. Milan said. Taking the advice to heart, she composed a poem that began this way.

> Just as I am, without one plea but that Thy blood was shed for me,
>
> And that Thou bidd'st me come to Thee, O Lamb of God, I come, I come!

In 1849 William Bradbury set the words to music. Since then it has become one of the most beloved hymns of all time. For many years, Billy Graham has ended all his crusade sermons with the singing of "Just as I Am." The third verse contains Charlotte Elliott's own testimony:

> Just as I am, though tossed about, with many

a conflict, many a doubt.

Fightings and fears within, without, O Lamb of God, I come, I come!

And the last verse contains the gospel promise:

Just as I am, Thou wilt receive, wilt welcome, pardon, cleanse, relieve;

Because Thy promise I believe, O Lamb of God, I come, I come!

That is also the promise God makes to you and to me. If you will come—just as you are—and if you will believe the gospel promises, He will welcome, pardon, cleanse, relieve. May that be your experience as you come by faith to Jesus Christ, the great Lamb of God.

Chapter Nine

FIRST STEPS IN A NEW DIRECTION

Trusting Christ as Savior and Lord is the most important decision you will ever make. Your eternal destiny has been changed because of what Christ has done for you. But that is not the end of the story. In many ways, it is only the beginning.

Perhaps you have heard the term *born-again* and wondered where it comes from. Originally, the term came from the lips of Jesus. It describes the new life He gives to those who come to Him in saving faith. Just as physical birth ushers in a new life that leads to physical growth, being born-again spiritually produces in you a brand-new life that leads to spiritual growth.

Salvation in the biblical sense has three parts. First, you are saved from the guilt of sin in your past the moment you trust the Lord Jesus Christ. Second, you are being saved moment-by-moment from the power of sin in the present as you depend on the Lord and obey His commands. Third, you will be saved from the presence of sin in the future when you finally stand before the Lord in heaven. In that day, sin and its corrosive consequences will be removed from your life once and for all. While it is true that believers enjoy salvation now, the best is yet to come.

I began this book by promising you some good news that could change your life. Part of the good news is that once you trust Christ, your sins are forgiven, Christ comes into your life, you become a part of God's family, and you receive the gift of eternal life. You don't need to fear death, for when you die, you will go to heaven to be with the Lord Jesus forever.

At the end of a conference in Hudson, Florida, an older couple drove me to the Tampa airport so I could catch my flight back to Chicago. As we talked, the father shared a tragic story about the death of one of his sons at the age of thirty-three. It happened just as the son was completing his training to be a missionary. Cancer took him in death after only three months. Before he died, he encouraged his parents with these words, "Don't worry about me. I'm just being transferred to Headquarters." His parents have cherished those words ever since his death.

Where does that faith come from? What hope do any of us have of going to heaven? Surely it is this: Through faith we have been united with Jesus Christ.

When we die, we will be where Christ is, and we know where He is because forty days after He rose from the dead, the Lord Jesus Christ ascended into heaven. At the moment of death, the children of God can rest assured that the Christ who ascended bodily into heaven will take them to be with Him—and will one day raise their bodies immortal and incorruptible. This assurance is not just for a selected few believers, but it is meant for all those who come to Christ in genuine saving faith.

Another part of the good news is that Christ comes into your life to change it from the inside out. As He makes Himself at home in your heart, you will discover new desires you never had before and new strength to empower your new desires. The Christian life begins the moment you trust Christ, but it doesn't end there. It continues day by day as you learn to walk with God, to grow in faith and love, to pray to your heavenly Father, to follow Jesus wherever He leads you, and to share His love with those you meet. If the Christian life is a book, coming to Christ is only chapter 1.

Here are some practical tips that will help you along the way.

PERSONAL ASSURANCE

• Don't base your salvation upon how you feel at a given moment. Even the greatest Christians have seasons of doubt and uncertainty. Doubt can even be good if it leads you back to a new confidence in God and in His Word.

• Don't base your salvation on an experience or even on your own faith. Remember that faith itself is a gift of God. You are not saved by faith in Christ but by Christ who saves you through faith. Rest your hope on who Jesus is and what He accomplished for you in His death and resurrection.

• Since salvation is of the Lord, you don't need to base your relationship with Christ on a date or a time when you had a certain experience. You don't consciously remember the moment of your birth, but you know you are alive. You may not remember the precise moment of your spiritual birth into God's family, but the Holy Spirit will give you assurance as you continue to believe God's promises and trust Christ alone as your Savior.

SPIRITUAL GROWTH

• Just as physical growth happens slowly over time, the same is true in the spiritual arena. If you have struggled in some area before coming to Christ, it is altogether likely that you may continue to struggle in that area for some time to come. Pray about your problems. Find some other Christians to encourage you along the way. Be honest with the Lord about areas of your life that aren't changing as fast you would like. Use your struggles as an opportunity to grow.

• Jesus calls His followers *disciples*, which means "learners." Ask God every morning to help you follow Jesus all day long. Jesus also calls you to "take up your cross" daily, which means setting aside your own agenda to follow Christ.

• You will discover His agenda for your life through regular prayer, study of the Bible, by meditating on and memorizing key Scripture verses, and through the counsel of other Christian believers. All these things are part of the leading of the Holy Spirit, who now indwells you.

THE CHURCH

• One evidence of new life is that God gives you a love for other Christians. You certainly will grow much faster if you unite with a Bible-believing local church where the gospel is preached and Christians are challenged to serve the Lord. God never intended His children to be hermits, living in cocoons, separated from each other. You need to be part of a local church for corporate worship, following Christ in baptism, the regular experience of the Lord's Supper, fellowship with other Christians, and the opportunity to learn by listening to the teaching and preaching of God's Word. You also need the spiritual discipline of following godly leaders who can help you discover and use your spiritual gifts.

• God's heart embraces the whole world. Being part of a local church connects you to the worldwide Christian community. Through your church you will support missionaries in other countries and you will also learn of opportunities to unite with Christians in other churches in larger enterprises for the kingdom of God.

SPIRITUAL DISCIPLINES

• God gives His children a love for His Word. If you don't have a Bible, purchase one and begin to read it every day. Start with one of the Gospels (the book of John, for instance) and read the unfolding story of the life of Christ. Then make it a habit to read at least one psalm each day and also one chapter from the book of Proverbs.

• Most new believers discover that they gain much from being with a small group of believers on a regular basis. Here you develop friendships, find a place to get your questions answered, and share stories of how God is helping each of you day by day. Most local churches make some provision for this kind of ministry, either through classes on Sunday or through groups that meet in homes during the week.

• Today there is a wealth of resources available to help you grow. These include various translations of the Bible, study Bibles with notes, books that help you understand the Bible and the Christian life, and an abundance of Christian music. In addition, there are computer programs and Internet sites filled with useful information. If you don't know where to begin, visit a Christian bookstore near you and ask one of the staff to help you find some of these resources. Your church may have a lending library; this will also be a helpful source of books and tapes regarding Christian growth and Christian theology.

• Be sure to give God the first few minutes of every day. Take time to focus your heart and your thoughts on the Lord. You can do this through prayer, Bible reading, listening to good Christian music, and also by reading good devotional material that points you to the Lord and to His Word. The first few minutes are vital because they set the tone for the rest of the day. I suggest you keep a spiritual journal in which you write down key insights from Scripture and record the spiritual lessons the Lord teaches you through the circumstances of life.

• As you grow in Christ, you will find a new desire to share your material resources with others. Become a joyful giver. And how do you do that? By giving what you have to God. This certainly involves giving a portion of your money to the Lord through His church. You will also find many opportunities to give to those less fortunate than you. God loves a cheerful giver, but you can never experience that until you give joyfully from the heart.

TEMPTATION AND SIN

• Before too long you are certain to face temptation to sin. It will probably come at a moment when you don't expect it. Remember that temptation itself isn't a sin; it's how you respond that makes a difference. Whenever God allows you to be tempted, He also makes a way of escape. Pray for wisdom to see the way out and then ask God for courage to take that way when you see it.

• As you grow in your new life, the Holy Spirit will give you a desire to obey God and a growing hatred for sin. When you sin, you only have two choices. You can hide your sin and pretend it didn't happen, but if you do that, your life is certain to get worse, not better. Or you can confess your sin—admit what you did and ask God to forgive you. God blesses those people who confess their sin and ask for forgiveness. He will give you both the desire and the power to say no to sin as you rely on Him.

YOUR PERSONAL WITNESS

• It is natural for you to share your faith with others. Be bold in your faith. Don't let opposition silence your voice. Speak up for what you know is right. You may someday have to speak out against evil. Speak the truth in love and then trust God for the results. Your courage will bring you much joy and will encourage other Christians to be bold as well.

• Pray for opportunities to share the good news—the gospel—with others. Ask God to make you sensitive to those you meet each day. There are many ways to talk about Christ with someone else. You might want to buy an extra copy of this book and have it on hand so that you can give it to a friend. Ask your friend to read it and tell you what he or she thinks about it.

• Coming to Christ changes the way you look at the world. Those who follow Jesus are called to be His ambassadors in the world—doing justice, loving mercy, and helping those in need. Ask God each day to help you make a difference in the world. Small things done in Jesus' name can have a huge impact on others.

YOUR ATTITUDES

• Asking questions is great way to grow spiritually. As you study the Bible and as you listen to sermons and Bible studies, jot down your questions. See if you can find the answers on your own through your own personal study. If not, ask a friend or a trusted Christian leader to help you find the answers. Never be ashamed to admit you don't know something. That's always the first step in personal growth.

• Don't be surprised when hard times come. Jesus promised that in this world His followers would encounter much difficulty. God allows hard times to come in order to develop our faith, purify our motives, reorient our focus away from the things of the world, and enable us to grow spiritually. When those hard times come, pray for endurance so that your faith will not fail.

• Gratitude is another mark that you are a child of God. All that you have, including life itself, comes from God. Take time daily to say "Thank You" to God for all His blessings. This will keep you from becoming hard and bitter when things don't go your way.

GOD'S PLAN FOR YOU

• Look for a chance to serve the Lord in some practical way. You will discover that God has given you talents that will enable you to serve the body of Christ, His church. As you serve, you will find great fulfillment and deep joy in the Lord. Don't limit yourself to what you think you would like to do. Ask God to use you in the way He deems best.

• Remember that coming to Christ is not like taking up a new hobby. It's the beginning of a new life where you come to know the God who created you. Although you don't realize it now, God has started a lifetime project of making you like His Son, the Lord Jesus Christ. You aren't a finished product yet, which is one reason why the Christian life won't always be easy.

Becoming a Christian means taking a journey that starts on earth and ends in heaven. If you have gotten this far in the book, I believe you are well on your way in your journey with the Lord. Keep on moving forward, keep your eyes on the prize, and you will not be disappointed. In the spiritual life, direction makes all the difference. God is more interested in direction than perfection. Now that you have committed your life to Christ, there will be many surprises, some wonderful answers to prayer, and no doubt some major battles to fight. You may find yourself going up and down in your Christian life. If that happens, don't despair. Just keep on moving forward with Christ. Daily obedience is the key. The Holy Spirit will help you to obey the Lord.

Some days you may feel as if you aren't making any progress at all. Don't let your feelings rule your life. Trust God and keep walking in the right direction.

With that we come to the end of this book. If you haven't yet trusted Christ as Savior and Lord, I encourage you to go back and read chapter 8 ("Coming to Christ") again. The gift of God is eternal life through Jesus Christ our Lord. The gift is yours for the taking. This is the good news that can change your life.

If God gives us understanding of who Jesus Christ is and what He did for us, our only response can be to come to Him in love and trust, asking Him to save us. May God grant you faith to believe in Jesus Christ. If you have doubts, come and see for yourself. The way to heaven has been opened by the Son of God. Come just as you are, holding nothing back, making no excuses. Come, and as you come to Christ, He will come to you.

If you would like to contact the author, you can reach him in the following ways:

By letter: Ray Pritchard
Calvary Memorial Church
931 Lake Street
Oak Park, IL 60301

By E-mail: PastorRay@cmcop.org

Via the Internet: www.cmcop.org

Ray Pritchard (Th.M., Dallas Theological Seminary; D.Min., Talbot School of Theology) is senior pastor of Calvary Memorial Church in Oak Park, Illinois, where he lives with his wife and their three children. He is the author of such books as *Keep Believing*, *The Road Best Traveled*, and *The ABC's of Wisdom*.

Moody Press, a ministry of Moody Bible Institute,
is designed for education, evangelization, and edification.
If we may assist you in knowing more about Christ
and the Christian life, please write us without obligation:
Moody Press, c/o MLM, Chicago, Illinois 60610.